Teaching History

K.M. Shrimali
Vikas Gupta
Mahima Singh
Smita Sahgal
Pradeep Kant Choudhary
Shalini Shah

AAKAR

Teaching History
K.M. Shrimali, Vikas Gupta, Mahima Singh, Smita Sahgal, Pradeep Kant Chaudhary and Shalini Shah

First Published 2013
Reprinted 2024

ISBN 978-93-5002-243-6

Published by
AAKAR BOOKS
28 E Pocket IV, Mayur Vihar Phase I
Delhi 110 091, India
www.aakarbooks.com

Printed at
D.K. Fine Art Press, Delhi

Contents

From the Authors

The research papers included in this anthology are revised and extended versions of presentations made at Peoples Education Congresses organised by Peoples Council of Education. Established in 1995 and subsequently duly registered in 1998, this Council has, in the last nearly two decades, striven for a new democratic system of pre-University education. Under the inspiring leadership of Dr N.P. Chaubey, the First Peoples Education Congress on 'Science Communication' was held in Allahabad in September 2005 and the Second such Congress was held at Mumbai in 2009. A two-day Post-Congress Symposium on 'Science Education in India' was hosted by the School of International Studies in the Jawaharlal Nehru University Campus (New Delhi) in December 2009. All, except the last essay in this collection, were presented at this Symposium.

There are several running themes in these papers. While on the one hand, these essays are unpretentiously 'academic'; in more senses than one on the other hand, they are 'experiential' too. These essays are also documents of an interface between the teacher and the 'taught' wherein the latter includes both students and contents of the historical discipline. These interfaces are somewhat unusual pedagogic exercises. To illustrate, one of the authors goes straight from being a student at the postgraduate class to become a teacher, who handles young pre-secondary stage students and experiments with the problems of developing history syllabi for such students in the company of such people who bat with several pre-conceived and emotionally laden acquired concepts that are not rooted in observations based on empirical material. Then, there is a mother who grapples with challenges of helping a young son with his preparation of Social Studies (History, Civics, Geography) where the son's common refrain was "SST is a bore". Two other authors share their experiences of seeing the transition from school to the first year of the collegiate history training. And yet another contributor with several years of practical experience of teaching history at various schools in Delhi, brings out the neglected area of school-community interaction and militaristic kind of disciplinarian apparatus as well as perpetuation of nefarious class hierarchy in the class rooms.

The Symposium where most of these papers were presented was attended by several professional scientists. One such participant comprehended the 'scientific' in the sense of almost Engels' paradigm of the evolution of 'Family', 'Property' and 'State' marking the growth of humanity. Another participant said that people with background of 'social sciences' have a much wider perspective than 'scientists' and that 'scientific temper' is a term that is peculiar to India, for, it is not used elsewhere. Today, the centres of knowledge production in the public domain are raising question marks about 'science disciplines' being 'scientific'. Simultaneously, the onslaughts of neo-colonial powers on the teaching of 'social sciences' are sharpening as can be seen in the current debate on the structural changes in the undergraduate programme of the University of Delhi. In such an academic ethos, discussing parameters of 'scientific history' would certainly be considered a hazardous venture. And yet, most of the contributions being presented here do precisely that, though with subtle nuances and by allaying the deeply engrained stereotypical ideas about 'physical/natural sciences' and 'social sciences' in the young teen-aged minds.

For the first contributor, scientific engagement means the need for being sensitive to students' multiple identities – need to avoid students' alienation; and at the same time, enabling and promoting students to rationally unpack historical narratives. Another contributor discusses epistemological bases of natural sciences and history and finding too many variables in human-nature inter-action concludes: "Writing a scientific history is easier said than done. In dealing essentially with the question of identity, history writing has been volatile, often a victim to assault. It is human nature to disagree and make sure that one's opinion is heard. But every polarity of thought is another step towards a fresh understanding and the building of a wider knowledge base." For two other contributors, 'scientific engagement' must be rooted in the cultural milieu of the child as pedagogical exercise and in the learner-centric system for producing knowledge. Putting it somewhat differently, scientific engagement of communicating history also lies in locating 'crossroads' in a class and recognising social diversities in the class room. A student, after studying history in the first year of the collegiate programme at the undergraduate level, unabashedly and unambiguously claimed: "I proudly call history a scientific discipline because it permits itself to be questioned and does not take a stubborn recourse to stating that it reveals nothing but the absolute truth".

Under the garb of studying 'popular culture' and perhaps also under the influence of the *avant-garde* 'post-modernism' there has been, since the turn of the millennium, a growing trend to underplay the dynamics of India's social fabric. Intense debates on history syllabi for school education epitomised in National Curricula Frameworks from 2000 onwards have shown that the accent therein is only on the narrative elements in communicating history. The paramount need of focusing on 'explanation' of historical processes (howsoever subjective such an exercise may be) is completely sought to be abhorred. Historians cannot allow the historical discipline to degenerate to the extent that the distinction between myth and history is lost and false history becomes instrumental in promotion of political mythology. The *raison d'etat* of history teaching and writing is reason and not faith.

Notwithstanding that all history is hypothesising and is

entirely interpretive and recalling Geoffrey Barraclough's famous dictum that 'history is not factual at all, but a series of accepted judgements', the following essays uniformly underline the centrality of 'causation'. Since no history can conclude with 'hence proved', like in Boolean algebra, with one definitive explanation for the past, the historian tries to look for consistencies in human thought across time and space to make humankind's evolutionary processes more intelligible. Uni-dimensional determinism has no place in any history teaching that claims to be 'scientific'. Instead, 'scientific engagement' in teaching history is located in the recognition of the multi-facetedness and non-absoluteness of 'Truth'; and in enhancing critical faculties of students by training them to ask questions, even at the risk of incurring the wrath and violence of the most devout and believer in the 'sacred'. The ultimate goal of teaching history is to produce a 'thinking mind' and a 'thinking being'. Is that the reason why this discipline is in the direct firing line of the neo-colonial powers?

We gratefully acknowledge the generosity of Dr N.P. Chaubey, the moving spirit behind Peoples Council of Education, for providing us the forum to share our ideas on the subject. We also thank Shri K.K. Saxena of Aakar Books for ungrudgingly accepting to publish this monograph and bringing it out expeditiously.

K.M. Shrimali
Vikas Gupta
Mahima Singh
Smita Sahgal
Pradeep Kant Choudhary
Shalini Shah

July 27, 2013

1

Learning Scientific History in Schools: An Insider's Account

Vikas Gupta

Introduction

Theorists of education have repeatedly cautioned us against the belief in the neutrality or objectivity of the aims of educational enterprise. Despite a number of differences amongst scholars, particularly in terms of their focus on the role of any specific class and the degree to which it can determine the nature and outcome of education, this has been one of the central points of agreement in the Western sociology of education.[1] Studies on the social aspects of education in India also validate this point.[2] Yet it has been virtually an omnipresent or ubiquitous tendency to present 'mainstream schooling' as something which is (and which supposedly should remain) aloof from' subjective' concerns of people and groups in society. It thereby implies—in an illusory fashion—espousing or adhering to the idea of education for its own sake: something non-political, immune from all kinds of struggles of people in the larger society, for these are then seen as the elements, which may pollute the very essence of education itself. As soon as these struggles and concerns—even the idea of asserting and nurturing cultural identities of various kinds—are explicitly made to impinge on the domain of educational enterprise, it is assumed that this is no more education.[3]

The controlling agencies of education (generally supportive of stalemate in the social order)[4] attempt to restrict schooling to the dissemination of "official knowledge" alone, even though this body of knowledge is essentially selective and for that reason necessarily subjective or laden with specific value judgments.[5] However, the other ('peripheral') knowledges are marginalised not through their complete suppression, but rather by subsuming them within the hegemonic framework of "official" or ('authentic') knowledge.[6] Besides employing other strategies, the hegemonic agencies controlling education achieve this task by keeping the system inflexible to provide no scope for the adoption and realisation of innovative radical ideas generated in alternative educational practices or in the context of the struggles going on in the civil society.[7] The subordinate groups too, however, do not accept this hegemonic knowledge without resistance: even they reject it in creative ways; but this rejection also contributes in the reinvigoration of social hierarchies.[8] In this scenario, school, an instrument of the dissemination of "official knowledge" does not recognise the validity of the experiential knowledges of learners even as the starting point of any pedagogic inquiry, which perpetuates the disjunction between official knowledge and outside reality.

Hence, the argument proposed in this paper is that it is a serious political and pedagogic requirement to ensure a more systematic interaction between school and students' cultural milieu; between "official knowledge" and other forms of knowledges; and between state and community. By drawing on educational theory, historical epistemology, and the author's first hand experiences of engagement with school students as a social science teacher,[9] this paper illustrates systemic limits of the dominant paradigm of classroom learning to promote scientific learning of society.

It, therefore, underlines the need to restructure the system by ensuring student teacher and parent interaction; pedagogic exchange between school and outside community; and teaching methodology in consonance with these objectives. The paper seeks to scrutinise social science learning through an examination of the pattern of history education in schools by situating it in the broader context of historical and educational theory, constrains on teacher's agency, informal one-way influences of outside cultural milieu on classroom transactions and the absence of formal pedagogic intervention of school in the pattern/processes of community socialisation of children.

This paper suggests that for students' orientation in history as a science of interpreting the traces of past events, it is essential that besides familiarising students with historical knowledge, there should be equal—if not greater—focus on training them in historical methods and inculcating in them an aptitude for historical inquiry or interpretation. It suggests that students' own lived experiences or concrete life situations may be used in order to initiate them in the field of historical inquiry. To what extent is it possible in the currently dominant paradigm of schooling? This is the question analysed in detail in the second half of this paper through the author's own experiences of teaching in schools. The first half of the paper sketches an outline of the child's cultural milieu, the nature of history as a component of social sciences and the position of the teacher whose agency is pivotal in the learning process.

I

School, Community and the Child's Cultural Milieu

Besides school, the community is another powerful element of children's socialisation. However, the community is far from something homogeneous; and even the term has multiple connotations in various social, administrative and spatial contexts. Sometimes it is used in the sense of religious (communal) or social (such as caste), where till quite recently, discussion of these entities with reference to education was more or less unanimously considered by scholars as something essentially obscurantist and therefore opposed to the ideals of secularism and liberalism.[10] It is despite the fact that these entities have been successfully affecting education with their preferences, biases and inclusions/exclusions.[11]

On the other hand, the term community is being readily used these days in the discourse on education, where by and large, it implies locality. In such discussions, the role of community (implying local population and administration) in education is conceived largely in terms of the need to claim locally available resources and to enlist the participation of local people in certain managerial tasks associated with schools primarily with the view to improve access to education or with the objective of "empowerment" of community.[12] Evidently, it too falls short of adequately focusing on the pedagogic interaction between school and community, or the community as a source of knowledge production.

However, the National Curriculum Framework (2005) underlined epistemic and pedagogic significance of 'local' and experiencial, which triggered a debate amongst scholars on the question of the place of 'local' in 'national'.[13] Nevertheless, this essay attempts to build on pedagogic and cognitive vitality of 'local' in the learning process of children without surrendering or considering it as necessarily antithetical to 'national'; but it agrees with the suggestion to ensure adequate safeguards against the encroachment on 'scientific reason' while using 'local'.

Since the term community has multiple connotations, it may also refer to the conglomeration of people attached with particular professions, or community of particular cultural performers/artists. These may be both, local as well as translocal. The term community is also used simply to refer to the child's cultural milieu outside the school boundary.[14]

The child's cultural milieu comprises various elements, such as his/her family, community and natural as well as built habitat. Foremost of these components is the role of family in the socialising process of children, and its influence in determining the nature and degree of students' participation in school. This theme requires more systematic and in-depth study than what is offered in this paper. Nevertheless, its impact can be seen at different levels in this essay, which offers significant clues to understand why engaging with family socialisation is important for school, which the latter relentlessly and constantly tends to relegate out of its concerns.

Another component of the child's cultural milieu is the natural and built habitat, which consists of many things including earth forms, (water, air, flora and fauna), and built structures (houses, historical monuments and markets), which may be useful in the learning process of students, particularly because children learn better with concrete objects than abstract concepts. There is another component of children's milieu outside the school, which has acquired immense influence over children's understanding, e.g. media, particularly the electronic one.[15] Therefore, the present paper provides a broad framework to ponder over the question how teachers can use these resources in children's learning process in the present pattern of schooling?

Three models have been suggested to distinguish the ways in which national systems of education negotiate the home-school binary. These are "complete overlap model", "complete discordance model" and "negotiated intersection model."[16] It has been argued that the ambivalence of the Indian education system keeps it in the second model, because the school system while emphasising the national or constitutional objectives does not allow the students and the teachers to refer to the child's cultural milieu. This weakness is evident both at the level of national policy and in everyday classroom practices.[17]

The discordance between school and children's cultural milieu is an intricate phenomenon, for there may be differences in the ways students experience this discordance, or in the degree to which this discordance alienates them from each other and from school itself. Cultural symbols of the 'mainstream' still make inroads through various channels but other cultures in this process are marginalised in school. Schooling therefore implies differential experiences and outcomes for students of different socio-cultural backgrounds.[18] Despite the prevalence of this discordance, the dominant trends of the outside world affect the nature of schooling, but school as a consciously transformative institution does not move out of its physical confines to interact with the outside community in order to transform it and to use it as a pedagogic resource in the learning process of students.

Yet, the argument sketched above about the disjunction between school and cultural milieu of learners may prove useful to explore further the pedagogic implications of this divide. However, before we investigate these issues further with reference to social science learning in schools with the example of history education, let us here spend some time in outlining the nature of history: an important component of social studies or social sciences.

History and Science

This section will take up some fundamental questions about the nature and relationship of history and science: their changing character, their driving force, the nature of scientific and historical truth and some theoretical issues in the teaching of history at school level. This is essential as a prelude to the analysis (carried out in the following sections) of the pattern of teaching and learning of history in the schools.

Ginzburg had suggested that in the pre-Renaissance period a distinction existed between the "high" and "low" forms of knowledge, which also corresponded with the distinction between the moral and intellectual pursuits of inquiry. For example, cosmic reality: it was forbidden to look into the skies, as well as into the secrets of nature. Religious reality: it was forbidden to know the secrets of God. Political reality: it was forbidden to know the secrets of the mysteries of politics. However, it started changing from the Renaissance onwards. Moreover, in this period, the natural or physical sciences began to acquire prestige as a separate discipline and became even more reputed than other forms of inquiry.[19] For instance, men like Galileo or Kepler did not hesitate to look at the skies, even exploiting such new artificial devices as the telescope. Ginzburg's Sacardino was used to saying, "Only fools believe that hell does exist."[20] We find that many suppositions or long held truths of sciences, medicine and cosmos were radically altered, rejected or redefined in the period of the Renaissance and Enlightenment.

Thomas Kuhn has also suggested that the history of science could be analysed by recognising that in different historical periods there were dominant sets of assumptions which guided scientific thought. These assumptions characterised the paradigm and controlled what was valid or true at that time. Paradigms changed when the assumptions of the old paradigm ceased to be able to explain the majority of what was being observed.[21]

Hence, we can infer from these positions that instead of necessarily being absolute and eternal, scientific truth is non-absolute, contingent upon an overwhelming (but not necessarily complete) agreement amongst the experts situated in specific temporal and social contexts and therefore subject to change. Moreover, the driving force of natural or physical sciences is not exceptionally different from social sciences: it is the force of debate and disagreement amongst the practitioners, which decides, validates as well as modifies the truth; and which, in due course of time, leads to further progress in respective disciplines. Even within a given period, new researchers come up with fresh hypotheses and try to prove them with their observations and experiments; critique others conclusions with different methodologies and data; and thus differ from other practitioners of the same field.

There is more or less a general tendency to perceive scientific methods and techniques more authentic over others. However, even this is not an ahistorical social characteristic: it came into being at a particular historical juncture. "It was during the Enlightenment era that the new science – that is, mathematics, empiricism, observation and experiment – had won the battle against deductive reasoning, superstition, (sic) myths and metaphysics."[22]

Similarly, with reference to the changing nature of the discipline of history, we can say that historians are also no longer restricted to the discussion of the deeds of great kings; they are increasingly turning towards what their predecessors passed over in silence, discarded, or simply ignored.[23] Moreover, over the years, or may be over the centuries, historians have also rejected, modified or altered various old historical 'truths'. In fact, many scholars have demonstrated that what we generally understand as history today is merely one kind of historical tradition. Many other forms of historical traditions existed in various parts of the world during the pre-modern era, but with the growth of Western imperial hegemony, the Western style of history became the dominant one.[24] In the recent years, Indian historians have become interested in the study of those varieties of historical traditions, which were either replaced by the hegemonic Western style of recording past events or in some ways survived till contemporary times outside the domain of modern secular and rationalist history writing.[25]

Even within the Western tradition, there have been

different schools of opinions ranging from objective history to the rejection of history as being merely and essentially fictional.[26] Another position is that history is neither a bundle of facts nor a fiction; it is narratological.[27] Even when defined in this manner, historical narrative retains its distinct identity as all kinds of narratives (movies, novels, TV serials, stories, museums and monuments) have their own specificities and differences without necessarily privileging one over the other.

Moreover, this emphasis on history as a narrative should not signify the "death of the author", for he/she is like an architect, who by way of constructing a particular type of building, at least creates the possibility of various types of usage to which it is subsequently put. The 'author' is important by way of his/her particular choice of facts, because facts in history have a special significance: a sheer presence or absence of a fact can change the connotation of the narrative. For this reason, we cannot set aside the 'author' in deconstructing any narrative. Yet, at the same time, we cannot deny that active readers can read a text different from each other and at variance with the 'author' itself. Therefore, historical work may be dealt with as a verbal structure in the form of a narrative prose discourse that classifies past structures and processes in order to explain what they were by representing them as models.[28] A historian takes events that have happened and tries to provide an explanation: an argumentative structure. He/she answers questions by three different types of explanations: "Emplotment", "Argument" and "Ideological implication."[29]

Consequently, history plays a very significant role in different ideological mobilisations. According to Hobsbawm, it is a raw material for nationalist, ethnic or fundamentalist ideologies. "Past is an essential element, perhaps the essential element, in these ideologies. If there is no suitable past, it can always be invented."[30] Though history is a dialogue between the past and the present, the present cannot be allowed to pollute the historical narrative, for that interference will end up in producing nothing but anachronistic and ahistorical accounts.[31]

Through an analysis of British policy documents on education, Robert Philips discusses the relation of history with the state and how in the late twentieth century the latter has become keener to determine the course and nature of history taught in the schools.[32] Though his argument about the state's increasing desire to interfere in the selection of history is convincing, it appears that he has pitched the argument of the non-interference of the state in the selection and teaching of history in the preceding period too much. The preoccupation of the state to influence the nature of education (which also includes history) as documented by various scholars is a phenomenon which started much earlier with the beginning of the transition to modernity, not only during the last quarter of the twentieth century. It is closely linked with the transition from various kinds of social arrangements to state-sponsored or at least state-controlled system of education. It may be possible that the battles over history in particular and over education in general have become more public in Britain (as well as in India) during the last quarter of the twentieth century replacing the earlier situation where government's narrative was although very powerful, but the coverage of its contestation was not so extensive in the media.

The emphasis on interpretation in the history curriculum at the school level is seen as a bulwark against the dangers of ideologically slanted school history. Penelope Harnett shows that the recognition of the abilities of pupils that they could work as historians, asking similar questions and using similar sources of evidence began to emerge in the 1970s, influenced by J.S. Bruner's belief that pupils could learn the structure of any subject, provided it was introduced to them in a meaningful way that was appropriate to their stage of development.[33] It was expected that teachers would present different interpretations of controversial topics, which would encourage pluralism and democratic values. The emphasis on interpretations was also motivated by a belief that school history made insufficient use of secondary sources, and particularly the work of academic historians. However, it was also clarified that interpretations should not be exclusively restricted to historiography. Moreover, the emphasis on interpretation should not overstress the provisional nature of knowledge; instead, it should focus on the use of contextual knowledge.[34]

The discussion above should make it clear that although in some ways, history is different from natural sciences, both still share important traits. In terms of their driving force (learned disagreement) and nature of truth (non-absolute/non-eternal), both natural or physical sciences and history have a lot in common and are capable of contributing to each other. Therefore, the emphasis on learning scientific history is about enhancing the analytical faculties of students to deconstruct historical narratives in order to progress towards truth, which in itself is nothing necessarily absolute and fixed. Hence, the prime focus in such a definition should be on the habit of critical thinking and free inquiry, which is similar to the overall aims of education as articulated by various thinkers/philosophers of education as well.

The objective of learning scientific history is to grasp the historical nature of various phenomena and events instead of preserving belief in their givenness. This involves a proper understanding of space and time in history and different notions of time as well. Learning scientific history is a method of enabling the student's mind for methodically imagining, hypothesising and proving various phenomenon with evidence. It demands adherence to the secular way of thinking and rejection of the belief in the eternity of religious, racial, and class distinctions of society.[35] Therefore, instead of conceiving it as an end in itself, scientific engagement with history should be understood as a means in the training of students in critical thinking. It should enable students to become all the more inquisitive and prepare them in the habit of pursuing systematic inquiry.

Therefore, besides acquiring basic facts,—which is undoubtedly an important foundational pillar—another important requirement is the emphasis on interpretation. It, however, presupposes the acceptance of the recognition that historical work is a kind of narrative account and the discipline of history is a science of interpreting the traces of past events; and that the students are capable of scientifically engaging with it provided they get adequate opportunities, guidance, freedom and facilities.[36] In this view of history, every trace of past events is questionable and therefore treated as a problem. In fact, only in this way, even at school level, it can claim the status of social science.

For learning scientific history, it is also essential that textbooks provide some sense of decision making by the historian in writing his/her historical narrative: how has the historian(s) culled this or that information from his/her sources? Engaging with the following questions may prove fruitful in our attempt to examine the potentials of scientific teaching in schools. Whether history textbooks are designed and taught in a scientific manner or do they simply transmit the facts and events? Do the textbooks familiarise students with diverse viewpoints/perspectives of different ideological and socio-cultural groups in society? Whether the textbooks present history as an exciting mode of inquiry instead of as a frozen subject akin to revealed truth?[37]

Transacting the Textbook: Teachers' Agency?

In this section, besides textbooks, focus would also be on teachers, the pivotal agency of education. For, it is difficult to imagine any scope for scientific learning of any discipline, including history, if they continue to function as "meek dictators" or enjoy a "weak position"[38] in our system and remain a "missing link" of our policy formulations.[39]

Although the focus of the present essay is not so much on the contents of curricular knowledge rather its delivery and negotiation in schools, we cannot brush aside the former aspect altogether in our present discussion. Differences in various series of textbooks surely exert influence on the classroom activities; yet one should also consider a different question. Can a specific series of textbooks have the potentials to transform the nature of classroom transactions within a particular system?

As has been said above, differences in textbooks influence the nature of classroom transactions.[40] For example, if I think about the nature of classroom discussions, or the "frame" of curricular transactions through the previous NCERT (National Council for Educational Research and Training) textbooks on one hand and the SCERT (State Council for Educational Research and Training) Delhi textbooks and new NCERT textbooks on the other, the difference between them was surely noticeable.[41] It is possible to suggest on the basis of personal observations that as compared to the previous textbooks of NCERT, the SCERT (Delhi) textbooks and the new NCERT textbooks were more interesting for students and teachers, provided (relatively speaking) greater scope for self-learning for students and granted some space for local issues and environment.

Occasionally, these textbooks also attempted to sensitise students about the sources of history writing, the nature of historical evidence and "historian's craft". Further, instead of presenting a chronological capsule, a more or less unbroken series of facts and gist of complex interpretations of historical events summarised by the historians, these textbooks made perceptible efforts to follow (though not in a completely successful manner) the "unit approach" in order to possibly deal with the problem of 'knowledge explosion'.

Sometimes, these textbooks also referred to different intellectual positions on particular issues. Even at times these compelled teachers and the students to read something additional, because there were questions, for which no readymade answers were provided within the textbooks. Questions in these textbooks were given not only at the end of the chapters; but rather these were interspersed within the main texts as well, which had greater potential of engaging the students and the teachers in discussion. The SCERT (Delhi) textbooks also attempted to give some space to the discussion of religious ideas and personalities within a broadly secular historical framework. These textbooks, particularly those prepared and published by SCERT (Delhi) offered a treatment to different themes in such a manner that it brought out conflict in society in more unequivocal terms than ever before. A positive influence of the progressive approach of Eklavya was discernable in these textbooks.[42]

There were many chapters on the history, society, economy, geography and polity of the national capital in the textbooks of social science published by the SCERT of Delhi. However, teachers in the classroom discuss all this knowledge about the city, and sometimes even the locality, of these students largely through the textbooks. At best, teachers can occasionally use maps, charts, datelines and photographs as teaching aids. However, the present set-up of schooling hardly enables and rarely inspires teachers to use the outside community as a pedagogic resource in the learning process of students to help the latter understand their city in the ways that it may lead to the arousal of their consciense rather than to sheer memorisation of certain facts for examination purposes. How can the textbook-centred classroom-based learning activities motivate the students for critically thinking about various problems of their city when the immensely rich historical heritage of Delhi is thus left unused as a pedagogic source of learning the value of pluralism as the basic essence of its society?

For quite some time, curriculum planners in India have observed that the pedagogic use of outside resources (natural, social, economic and historical) in the formal learning process of students is necessary for various reasons.[43] Yet, there has been no change in this scenario despite a number of other reforms. The absence of regular, conscious and formal arrangements for pedagogic interaction between the school and the outside community reproduces the pattern of over-reliance on the textual or official knowledge and the rhetorical emphasis on the role of the teacher as the distributor of this knowledge.

After constructing a framework of analysis so far sketched in this paper (including an outline of some fundamental limitations of the present paradigm of schooling), we may now turn to make certain observations about the pattern of history learning in schools. It is based on the author's own experiences with the students.

Time, Space, Imagination and History

It was stated above—in the section on "History and Science"—that scientific engagement with history implies the ability to situate and comprehend historical events and phenomena in terms of their specific historical time and space. Else, it would become something ahistorical. It is elaborated here in the light of recent research and school experiences in order to assess the potentials of the present pattern of learning in schools to fulfil this essential requirement of scientific engagement with history.

The concepts of 'time and imagination' have a central place in the development of a child's historical understanding. Time is the distinctive marker of history, setting it apart from other disciplines based on the interpretation of evidence. For historical evidence itself derives its meaning from the timeframe in which it is set. Without a grasp of the concept of time, there can be no real understanding of change, development, continuity, progression and regression.

In a survey of the recent researches on this issue, William Stow and Terry Haydn argue that young children struggle to understand these abstract markers of time.[44] They suggest that the development of the concept of time is inextricably bound up with proficiency in language, and grasping the time sense becomes difficult for pupils because of another reason, namely that we have a wide range of different systems for describing time. Through a review of the arguments of various scholars, (Oakden and Sturt, Levstik and Pappas, Thornton and Vukelich, Lynn, Harnett, and Stow, etc.), Stow and Haydn suggest that the cultural and educational context influences the pace at which a child develops an understanding of the language of time.[45]

Further, Stow and Haydn identify a downward shift in the age at which children demonstrate this (chronological) aspect of understanding. They suggest that recent research on children's understanding of time has tended to move away from the idea of age-related models such as those of Piaget.[46] However, there have been different arguments and approaches over the appropriate ages at which children should be taught about various periods. In India, the remoter segments are studied by younger children, while older children study the more recent past. This sequencing of the subject matter of history has been seen as problematic in the context of the development of time sense in children. Therefore, one perspective has been that the focus should be from more recent to distant time in the teaching of history to children, because they can relate better with the time nearer to their own.[47]

On the other hand, Stow and Haydn make a different point. According to them, as opposed to the images and costumes of the Victorian era or 1940s, children at Key Stage 1 could look at the Romans as a period of time where almost everything would appear markedly different from today. In numerical terms, an understanding of the time of the Romans would be beyond Key Stage 1 children, but then they are not comfortable with numbers over one hundred at that age in any case. What might be clearer to them, in this instance, is the distinction between the past and the present. This distinction may not be so clear to the children with reference to more recent events.[48] However, in India, although the remoter past is studied by younger children, the focus in curriculum and examination has not been on curiosity and interpretation: overall focus has been on memorisation, instead of comprehension.

In the middle of the very first academic session of my teaching career, the vice-principal requested me to teach history to the students of 11th and 12th standards, because their teacher had gone on long leave. While teaching the students of the 11th class, one day I observed that they were not clear about the distinction between B.C. and A.D./CE; about different notions of time and about the use of dateline in the teaching of history. I wondered how they had studied history for so many years without knowing something so basic! Then I also talked to the students of junior classes on the same issues with the view to find whether the lack of understanding of these fundamental tenets of history amongst the students of the 11th class was an accidental feature, or if it could be regarded as representative of a wider phenomenon. To my utter dismay, I soon discovered that it was a general pathology.

I then decided to encourage students of all grades to think, inquire and write essays about the difference between B.C. and A.D. How it became the dominant pattern as a dividing line in the chronological arrangements in historical writings and whether there have been other ways of arranging chronology in diverse historical traditions? I even announced some prizes for the best essays. They were given full freedom to get this information from wherever they desired.

Finally, from the entire student body of that school, about two dozen essays were received: all of them from the students of junior grades. Some of the essays were truly good. However, when the students were asked for clarifications on specific points during presentations, it became apparent that most of the good essays were dictated by the private tutors or elders in the family or neighbourhood. Finding no way out, the essay was accepted if the student understood the meaning of what he/she had written. Finally, three students, whose essays were better than others were awarded without assigning first position to any one of them.

This entire exercise may be treated as another testimony of the problem of non-comprehension: the students pass on to the senior grades without even grasping the basics. Non-comprehension or poor achievement is an important challenge of school education. It has been interpreted in terms of various factors, such as an over-emphasis on bookish learning for ill-planned examination system, dull teaching methodology, curricular marginalisation of certain groups, infiltration of social prejudices to the school, economic deprivation, and teacher absenteeism and so on.[49] Any exploration of this problem of non-comprehension should also consider it in terms of the limitations on the agency of teacher and the disconnect between students' milieu and classroom, a situation which compels students to learn through abstract concepts, instead of learning from living reality.

This exercise clarified the significance of the idea of learning little but learning well,[50] as well as the superfluous nature of the official position against the report of the Yashpal Committee on curriculum load.[51] The nature of participation in this exercise may also be taken as an example of how the society and particularly the education system causes the slow death of curiosity and its replacement by reluctance in the student mind as they become older: my senior students did not take part in this exercise.

This exercise rendered it clear that these students might have been asked about other calendrical systems and notions of time, because in their families, for cultural reasons, they use different calendars. Amartya Sen has rightly suggested that the study of calendars and their history, usage and social associations can provide a fruitful understanding of important aspects of a country and its cultures. For example, since calendars often have religious roles, there is sometimes a clear connection between regional religions and domestic calendars. Indeed, even the global calendars of the world are often classified as 'Christian', 'Muslim', and 'Buddhist' and so on. The connection between calendars and cultures, however, goes well beyond this elementary linkage. Since the construction of calendars requires the use of mathematics as well as astronomy, and since the functioning and utilisation of calendars involves cultural sophistication and urbanity, the history of calendrical progress can tell us a lot about the society in which these developments occur.[52] Sen documents many instructive examples of cultural interaction and tolerance in the Indian subcontinent through a brief history of calendars. However, it is hardly a feature of the dominant paradigm to use the elements of the cultural milieu of students—calendars in this case—as a pedagogic resource in the formal learning process.

The imagination of time is not uniform amongst peoples and cultures across the globe or in different historical periods.[53] Therefore, another requirement stated above—in the section on "History and Science"—was the need to facilitate the opportunities of imagination, doubt and hypothesis development and its validation in order to promote school level students for critically thinking about historical dimensions of any phenomenon. However, to what extent is it possible to adhere to this norm in the present apparatus of school education?

One day I was taking a joint class of the two sections of the seventh grade, because a colleague was absent. The principal had asked me to combine that section since a high power delegation along with the wife of the then President of the World Bank was about to visit the school. Being the social science teacher of both these sections, I decided to do the regular business of teaching, but in a way, which was not necessarily a permanent characteristic of my pedagogy owing to various constraints. We started a chapter on the polity of India during 700 to 1200 CE. There was a section on how people became kings in that era.[54] It was about different ways of acquiring kingship. I attempted to encourage students to share with the class their imaginations of kings; and their knowledge gained from stories or from other sources regarding various ways of acquiring kingship.

One by one, many students shared with the class their interesting ideas, which were noted on the blackboard. Thus, we prepared a list of the responses of students on the question of how a person could become king. We then decided to go back to the textbook and see how it matched with our list.

Tripta Wahi describes in detail how the use of stories in Eklavya textbooks of history may lead to confusion for the learner who may understand them to be real. Some times this danger is explicit because of the shortcomings of explanations in the textbook and sometimes the danger is caused by the possibility that the children may not realise the difference between history and story.[55] It may be suggested that besides a careful writing style of textbooks, a lot would depend on how the teachers transact the reading material with their students. Still some amount of risk is always present in such an approach as the students are not the passive learners and all texts are open for different kinds of readings by the readers. Nevertheless, this method of teaching history is indispensable particularly when the target group consists of children and if the objective is to enable them to hypothesize.

At the point when we were finalising our list of the ways in which a person could become a king, the high-powered delegation entered the classroom. Somebody from that delegation asked us, "What are you doing?" The principal asked me to answer this question in English as the delegation included some foreigners. The delegation was delighted to hear the summary of our activity: our particular way of engaging with history. One Indian woman in that delegation instructed the students to one by one repeat whatever they had told the class before their arrival about various ways of acquiring kingship. When we encouraged them, some students started repeating their stories. I translated students' responses to the guests in English.

Students were excited because they were interacting with foreigners for the first time in their lives. The delegation was also satisfied to observe that the students learned in very creative ways in this school. However, I could not express the personal anguish of a teacher before the delegation that it was not a general reality of schools in Delhi, instead an occasional event. In fact, very soon after the commencement of this exercise, the anxiety had arisen that it was going to be a time consuming activity. Moreover, an additional concern of teachers and students in such learning activities is that whatever they are doing in the class may not be asked in the exam.

As has been suggested above, scientific engagement with history implies that students should comprehend any event under study in the context of its particular geographical location and within its historical time. Maps are recommended as a teaching aid to help students to imbibe this tenet of historical consciousness. However, in the schools of the Directorate of Education (Delhi), teachers rarely used maps in their teaching. Whenever they did so, instead of guiding the students to find out places by giving individual students or their small groups adequate chances for explorations, they simply displayed maps in the classroom. Those teachers who attempted to follow a different practice were often branded as unsuccessful in maintaining the discipline.

Once the Principal removed my periods in the eighth standard from the timetable and allotted another section of the seventh standard to me. One of the reasons of her negative assessment was my particular way of using maps in the teaching of history. Although I could not use maps very regularly, whenever I used them, I would invite students in small groups to see the map closely and find particular places. I always tried to maintain some order in the classroom by ensuring that not more than 4 to 5 students come to the front at a time. It was still a significant challenge to the militaristic apparatus of classroom where collective tasks were hardly given to students. I, however, sometimes tolerated minor violations of this norm by allowing students to see the map even outside their turn. Granting this liberty to the students was necessary, because the interest shown by them in the map activity reflected their curiosity to learn. After all, such a curiosity is more important to preserve and promote than anything else.

When the students came in groups to see the maps, this accorded them the chance of collective learning: an important corrective to our exclusive focus on individualised learning. It at least temporarily challenged the classroom hierarchy evident in the sitting arrangements, where generally the socially privileged and so-called intelligent students occupy the front rows.[56] Otherwise, how would the students sitting at their respective places, particularly the backbenchers, meaningfully observe and grasp the minor details in the maps hanging on the wall?

However, the principal could not understand the logic of inviting some students in the front near the map. On the contrary, she always attempted to ensure that students sit properly in their respective seats and look at the map from there only. Since I did not abide by this norm of militaristic discipline, she decided about me (using her general parameter based on the common practice of displaying maps) that I was not capable of teaching the students of the eighth standard as the children are relatively grown-up and they leave their seats in the classroom creating a situation of compromise with discipline. However, this way of involving students in map activity, instead of simply displaying maps in the class, could have proved destructive for the classroom hierarchy. Although, this hierarchy is an important barrier in children's learning process, any attempts to even temporarily disrupt it were resisted.

Even though the principal would not have disapproved the organisation of map activities in this manner, there was very little chance that one could have regularly practised it anyway, because it really required more time and better student-teacher ratio. Still, there was another possibility, which largely remained unrecognised and unacknowledged. Very often, in the midst of discussion on any topic, individual students would spontaneously come to the map and discovered things on their own without any instructions/orders from the teacher. Even this was considered contrary to the standard image of a social science class.

The experiences cited in this section underline the urgency to adopt the practice of drawing upon the prior knowledge and the cultural milieu of the students in the teaching process, the necessity of relaxing the disciplinarian apparatus of schooling and the need to enable the teacher to determine the nature, pattern and pace of learning activities in accordance with the specific requirements of individual students. These experiences reveal significant constraints or obstacles in the path of meaningful learning thrown up by the very structure of schooling.

II

Conflict, Identity and the Learning of History

It was described in the foregoing section how difficult or impossible it is to fulfil even the basic requirements of scientific engagement with history, such as understanding historical events and concepts in terms of their respective time and space; and imagining or hypothesizing on historical issues within the dominant paradigm of classroom learning. Through a scrutiny of two incidents of history classes, this section underlines another essential requirement of scientific engagement with history, namely the necessity of carefully dealing with the issue of identity. This section would also cite examples of the influence of familial and communitarian socialisation of students in their classroom behaviour; and how these create the need to have regular interaction between school, family and community. It is followed by a brief examination of a few more limitations inherent within the present structure of schooling, which the students and teachers face in this regard.

The arguments sketched in this section are based on the supposition that an individual possesses multiple identities, horizontal and vertical; and depending upon the context, one identity may become more articulate and evident over others in the behaviour of a person.[57] These identities may be based on many things, such as caste, class, religion, gender, ethnicity, language, region, nation, ideology, or disability. Sometimes a person may develop even more temporary and fluid forms of identity vis-à-vis her immediate opponents, such as the identity of the bearer of a particular viewpoint or argument in the classroom. Hence, it is indispensable for teachers to abstain from the temptation of expecting exclusive allegiance of an individual to any particular institution or ideology. On the contrary, there is a need to recognise that a person is bound to have multiple allegiances, which may at times even conflict with one another. In such cases, there is a need to interact with these allegiances instead of simply crushing them with the steamroller of mainstreaming. It is also essential to ensure the students' opportunities to learn from conflicting viewpoints and identities in their formative years.

We were studying a lesson of history in the sixth standard.[58] In the topic on the rise of Islam, when we discussed the passage from the *Quran*, mention of meat[59] caused a reaction among a few Hindu students who uttered "chee chee" (shame shame). Although a large number of Hindus enjoy non-vegetarian food, vegetarianism is seen as the norm of dominant upper caste or brahmanical Hinduism.[60] A Muslim student named Kamal Uddin stood up to complain, "They are saying bad things about our God." He assumed that the disparaging reactions of his classmates to non-vegetarianism were directed to his religion, because this is a general criticism of Muslims amongst Hindus that they eat meat.[61] Thus, it is evident that like other classmates, Kamal Uddin brought with him to the classroom the societal knowledge about the identity of Hindus and Muslims. There are scholars of education, who have already suggested that even when the curriculum eschew any discussion of the conflicts taking place in the outside world, these still find their way into the classroom.[62]

At this point the bell rang, and another teacher was waiting at the door; and therefore the discussion was abruptly but temporarily halted. Nevertheless, it was told that the peer group discussion continued during recess about which I do not have details to offer here. However, after the school hours, on our way back home, Kamal Uddin met me and asked, "*Vo hamare dharm ke bare men aisi gandi baten kyon karte hain jab main unke dharm ke bare men kuch nahin bolta hun*?" (Why do they say such bad things about our religion when I do not say anything about theirs?)

The sense of identity was quite perceptible in Kamal Uddin's question as he used the terms "their" and "our" for Hindus and Muslims respectively. Nevertheless, another remarkable characteristic trait of children's personality was also evident in Kamal Uddin's interrogating approach, namely the desire to know, rather than the habit of taking sides in the conflicts relying on certain definitive assumptions about other religions and people belonging to them.

I told Kamal Uddin that most Hindus also relish meat, and therefore, the comments of your classmates may not necessarily be directed to your religion. This probably failed to satisfy him; and he most likely discussed the incident with the elders in the family or neighbourhood. (On other occasions in our personal conversations, Kamal Uddin often shared with me his habit of discussing various matters of his school life with his father.) The following day he taught me the highest level of religious philosophy. He said, "*Sabhi dharm acche hain aur sabhi dharm kharab hain.*" (All religions are good and all religions are bad.)

Before examining further the case of Kamal Uddin, let us look at another experience. One day, we were discussing in seventh standard the history of the Mughal period and in particular the reign of Aurangzeb.[63] The SCERT (Delhi) textbook of history attempted to present a secular interpretation of Aurangzeb's period by focusing on the political context of his struggle with the Sikhs. Further, instead of describing him as a fanatic, this textbook portrayed Aurangzeb as an emperor who was concerned to personally observe the norms of piety prescribed in Islam and thus set up himself as a model for emulation by his subjects. It appears that this textbook made a serious effort to counter saffronised accounts of medieval Indian history officialised by the NCERT textbooks of NDA (National Democratic Alliance) Government.[64]

Therefore, besides the study of Aurangzeb's concern for Islamic piety, I also wanted students to understand the political context of the tension between the Sikhs and the Mughal emperor. However, a Sikh student of class seven, named Jaspreet, challenged the secular interpretation—in this case officialised by the state government—of the differences between Sikhs and the Mughal emperor Aurangzeb. She pointed to the animosity between Sikhs and Aurangzeb by referring to a story along with a few other details not mentioned in the history textbook prescribed for her grade. Thus, she underlined the religious bigotry of Aurangzeb by referring to his fights with the Sikhs; and she told the class about the assassination of the Sikh guru by the Mughal emperor. Though this event was mentioned in the textbook,[65] Jaspreet added a few other details to prove her point. For example, she told the class that Aurangzeb fed parts of the dead body of the guru to the dogs. The source of information in her case, as she stated in the class, was a message inscribed on the walls of a gurudwara (place of worship in the Sikh religion), though in her intervention Jaspreet did not mention the name/place of the specific gurudwara.

This event is represented/remembered in a different way in the dominant Sikh tradition, which believes that the Sikhs in a daring manner managed to send the head of the guru to Anandpur and the remaining lower part of his body was cremated at Rakabganj (in Delhi) by Sikhs.[66] If whatever Jaspreet was saying was really written in some gurudwara, then we can safely assume that she would have been visiting such a place mostly in the company of her family members. Otherwise, she would have been only informed about it by her family members or acquaintances. It is also possible that she was representing a different tradition of Sikhism (adhered to by her family) instead of the dominant one.

Another possibility lies in the recognition that children find it not so easy to retain chronology in their memory.[67] In this case, since Jaspreet relied on her memory, she might have intermingled her societal knowledge of the later events, such as the atrocities of partition days with the episodes of Aurangzeb's period. Here it may be pertinent to note that at least the father of Jaspreet (as well as of Kamal Uddin) is not illiterate; and therefore he could have also provided this information (culled from some historical account) to her.

Despite some obscurity about the authenticity of certain aspects in Jaspreet's statements and the precise source of her information, the point about the mediation of societal knowledge in classroom transactions of official knowledge is sufficiently clear. Even if someone proves certain facts in Jaspreet's account as fallacious, the point that students use their information gathered from (and regarding) the outside society to make their classroom claims authentic would still stand.

I tried to explain to Jaspreet with examples that for a student of history, it is also essential to understand the nature of the source of information before arriving at any judgment and that there is evidence of Aurangzeb's donations to non-Muslim people and institutions as well. Therefore, the religious policy of Aurangzeb may also be seen in terms of two things: his notion of piety guided by Islam and his political context.

Following Jaspreet's account, many students shared with the class various stereotypes about Muslims, which outside society had transmitted to them. Most of these stereotypes were related to the assumption that Muslims are very rude; they possess a hardy and fanatic character; they marry many times and they produce more children. (I will reflect upon these remarks in the next section.) This thread also led us to the discussion of the divisive politics practised by the right wing forces, which in the name of religion and culture attempt to build a non-secular nation. We also discussed some points about how stereotypical opinions generate, circulate and reproduce in society.

However, there was no Muslim student in Jaspreet's section of the seventh standard. We do not know what would have happened if a Muslim student had been present in the class at that time. We can only speculate that in the case of the failure of the teacher to provide appropriate guidance, such a child would somehow swallow this as a bitter dose shifting the outward conflict inside. Alternatively, this might create the kind of situation that we witnessed in the case of Kamal Uddin, where classmates, teacher, parents, all got involved in the debate. It is therefore possible to argue that in the guidance of a teacher committed to scientific history of religious issues, such discussions may prove very useful for the entire class including Jaspreet, Kamal Uddin and any other student from religious minorities.

Students of both religious minorities or the majority community might not get another chance to discuss these things later on in their lives in such an open manner with the members of other socio-religious communities outside the school if they are denied this possibility—and more than that, the requisite training and orientation—in their formative years inside that institution, which has the responsibility to prepare future citizens of the nation. At the same time, it is pertinent to underline here that for various reasons—some of these have already been cited in this paper—neither such open discussions in the classroom nor the chances for students of personally discussing such queries with teachers are frequently available in schools.

It is clear from the examples of Kamal Uddin and Jaspreet that students are not the 'tabula rasa': they bring to the classroom their identity consciousness and their societal knowledge. However, with a very open mind (a characteristic rarely found amongst the elders), they articulate it against one and the other. The pedagogy of history cannot ignore this trait of student behaviour if the objective is to promote amongst the students the value of curiosity and healthy doubt, the core of scientific learning. Otherwise, it may further marginalise those students who would not receive sufficient chance of articulating and negotiating their identity consciousness and societal knowledge in the classroom. Thus, it would deprive the entire class of the opportunity of learning from their experiences and perspectives.

Nevertheless, both these debates—Kamal Uddin's and Jaspreet's—remained unresolved because we did not have the opportunity to go and see the wall of the gurudwara, where Jaspreet had read the above reported message. Similarly, it was not possible for us to examine the dietary pattern of the locality where this school is situated; and to understand and expose the reasons why (and why it should not have) the reference to meat eating has assumed communal significance. This limitation becomes even more restrictive, because students at this stage of their evolution learn more with the help of concrete things, instead of from the abstract phenomena. Moreover, teachers wonder about the validity of these queries and the utility of the need to resolve them as part of their official mandate, which is confined to the requirement of completing the syllabus and preparing students to answer some expected questions in exams. Even I could not or did not make serious efforts to interact with the family members of Kamal Uddin and Jaspreet. However, the question about interaction with the family members or parents of students will be elaborated in the next section.

At the same time, the examples of Kamal Uddin and Jaspreet should not imply continuance of the colonial understanding of India as a conglomeration of sentimental communities exclusive of each other. For, neither religion alone completely claims the identity consciousness of Indians; nor these identities are essentially exclusive of each other. In this long period from Hunter to Sachar, this is certainly one significant improvement in our understanding of Indian society. These examples may, however, be seen as good pointers of the level of sensitivity of the students' minds on issues concerning their religious/cultural identities and the importance of understanding the interaction between "official knowledge" and "societal knowledge" in the learning process of students.

The concern for sensitivity on the issue of identities—including the religious identities—need not be considered as necessarily anti-secular. The study of both "old" as well as "recent" debates on secularism in the Indian context clearly reveals that the constitutional meaning and even the practice of secularism in India does not mean antipathy to religion as such. Even the 'critics of secularism' as a doctrine for the state are largely concerned with ensuring—despite many internal differences amongst themselves—some recognition of the religious sentiments of people.[68] Moreover, secular and religious are not two binary exclusive categories; they instead shape each other.[69] According to Alam Khundmiri, secularism can be understood as that attitude of mind on "this worldly matters", which refuses to accept the division of humanity into religions, races or historical classes as final.[70] Further, as Talal Asad has clarified, secularism does not simply valorize the human and worldly "out there" as opposed to the otherworldly. Secularism posits a particular conception of the world ("natural" and "social") and of the problems generated by that world.[71] Hence, this understanding of secularism emphasises reason and rationality; and these characteristics are prerequisites for scientific learning of history as well.

School and the Outside Community

The preceding section demonstrated how the community or family socialisation exerts considerable influence on responses of students towards the ideas discussed in the classroom. Their responses are not shaped in isolation. Instead, they negotiate the ideas learnt in school within the authoritative structures of the outside community and the epistemological framework of societal knowledge. Their final responses in terms of assimilation/rejection depend on various factors. For example, with whom did the child discuss that issue outside the school and whether that source was more trustworthy than the teacher was? What was his/her point of view? Did the child get an adequate opportunity to verify the officially approved and transmitted idea by interacting with the people or community in question? Hence, final adoption of an idea, however rational and liberal depends on the opportunities of pursuing, refining and investigating it in the context of interaction with different socio-religious communities. However, as will be seen below, the interaction among socio-religious communities is not an invariably regular feature of the world outside the school; and presently schools, too, fail to provide any remedy for this situation. Is it not a serious limitation of the presently dominant paradigm of school education?

Once we were studying in the tenth standard the topic on "Challenges before Indian Democracy" and specifically the problem of communalism in India.[72] Though it was a different class and a different school, students were making almost the same kind of remarks about intercommunity relations between Hindus, Muslims and Sikhs, which we have already witnessed in the above-cited examples of Jaspreet and the classmates of Kamal Uddin. An addition was the assertion that "*Musalman atankwadi hote hain aur vo Pakistan ke prati wafadar hote hain.*" (Muslims are terrorists and their loyalties rest with Pakistan.)

These responses may be interpreted in terms of the dearth of interaction amongst socio-religious communities outside the school. I asked these boys how many of them were Muslims. I found that there were only two in the class of 35. Then I asked all the other students how many of them had the chance to have food or share a meal with the family members of these two students? I received no answer. I further asked, if they had ever visited a Muslim family? Only one student answered positively: "Just once sir."

Here the inclination is not to make any generalised statement about the nature and extent of intercommunity interaction for the entire country, because it may not have a uniform pattern. However, the specific picture that emerged out of this conversation about the pattern of interaction amongst urban families of different religious backgrounds, particularly in those parts of Delhi where most of these students resided, surely presented a challenge: in their familial world, these students (predominantly Hindu) did not experience interaction with members of Muslim families. In such a scenario, any unit of history on intercommunity relations would remain devoid of the advantage of real life experiences of the interaction amongst students of different religious communities. It would render the entire exercise as dependent on learning or memorisation of facts and interpretations from the book. It would continue to limit the possibilities of scientific understanding or critical learning about the diversity of society. How will this situation be reformed if the school too continues to shun this responsibility of ensuring—going out of its self-constructed prison of physical boundaries—that the students get adequate chances of intercommunity interaction?

The necessity of ensuring interaction between the cultural milieu of students on one hand and classroom learning on the other is significant for all students, coming either from marginalised or dominant cultural backgrounds.[73] It is a political as well as a pedagogic requirement for a liberating education: learning of history or any other discipline. One student of the 9th class named Avneesh was expected to sit for the compartment exam. However, he was planning to skip it in order to visit his native village with his parents to attend a *Janeu*[74] wearing ceremony. I could not convince him to change his (or his family's) decision. Any meaningful intervention in Avneesh's case required an active, constant and sustained process of dialogue with the parents, which is generally missing in the formal mechanism of schools.

Although, for various reasons, my personal efforts in the case of Avneesh did not yield positive fruits, it is still necessary to use such opportunities in the learning process of students. Teachers may use such situations, (which underline the importance of the sacred thread and the continuance of varna distinctions) to discuss the issue of caste inequalities and caste movements in both historical and contemporary contexts.[75] These situations may be used to draw the attention of students to those ceremonies, which help to maintain and "reproduce" the caste distinctions in society. Students may be invited to survey such events in their localities and native places, which might provide them opportunities for critically engaging with such varied topics.

However, it is not so easy for teachers in the presently dominant paradigm, either to meaningfully follow the "absence of frame" approach of choosing the topic for study according to the spontaneous situations; or to consider the "weak framing" as a viable option.[76] Involvement of teachers and students in creative learning outside the classroom is already a rare phenomenon. Further, any meaningful intervention in the case of Avneesh required an active, constant and sustained process of dialogue with the parents, which is generally missing in the formal mechanism of schools. 'Mainstream' schools do not make serious or meaningful attempts to establish any dialogue with the parents as if the latter exert no influence in the socialisation process of children. Schools leave parents and families out of the purview of their concerns as if the students will automatically imbibe all the democratic secular values which the school curriculum intends to develop amongst learners overcoming the trends of their familial or cultural socialisation (wherever they are at odds with each other); or as if the parents already and necessarily adhere and practise those values.

What Rabindra Menon wrote in 1959 is still unchanged. He wrote that "while in many advanced countries the home and the school are getting closer together and interacting for the benefit of children, here in our country no serious attempt has so far been made to get the home and the school to influence each other for the advantage of the child. The school and the home in India are separate worlds in themselves."[77] He said, "Much of the present dissatisfaction of parents in regard to schools and the reaction of despair in the mind of the teacher can disappear if the teacher, aware of the parents' picture of the school, tries to change it and paint a new and a truer one in its place."[78]

Menon in the above sentence rather casually placed all responsibility on the teacher. However, in the subsequent pages he was forced to underline teachers' limitations where he said that the kind of individualised attention by the teacher supposed above is not possible in the ordinary government schools. He contrasted these schools with those (private schools) where such parent-teacher interaction was practicable.[79]

Menon suggested, "While marks should be given and recorded, the progress report should be based on an observation of the student's home life (sic), his surroundings, his ability in class and should indicate in what way he has progressed or failed and what he requires if he is to show progress."[80] However, while suggesting so, he did not inquire if it is possible for a teacher in this kind of system? Nevertheless, Menon made an extremely important point. He said that if there is lack of harmony between what the child is taught at school and the experiences it has in the home, the sufferer will be the child.[81] He said, "Mere schooling alone is not education." He therefore suggested that schools should open home fronts in them and parents must be induced, if not compelled, to shoulder their responsibilities as co-educators.[82]

How can we expect the schools to have an active dialogue with the community outside it when even the already existing bodies for the interaction between the school and the parents of the students are almost dead? The Parent Teacher Associations (PTAs) exist only on paper; or such bodies very occasionally meet only in the ritualistic fashion to approve the operation of certain funds only. Parent Teacher Meetings (PTMs) hardly take place in these schools. Teachers meet parents of their students on very few occasions, such as while distributing school uniforms or scholarships; and sometimes to get their signature on the result cards.

Summing Up

Owing to the absence of a sustained process of dialogue between student, teacher, parent and outside community, (where teachers act in accordance with "the banking concept of knowledge"); and due to the failure of schools to empathise with (or ensure the pedagogic use of) the learner's concrete life experiences, the school becomes an instrument of enforcing pedagogic and cultural silence for all the learners notwithstanding possible differences in their experience of this divide and in the degree of their alienation because of their socio-cultural backgrounds.[83] In the policy recommendations of various committees and commissions on education in India, the relationship between the school and community has been recognised as the key to the solution of the ill-effects of examination-oriented bookish knowledge imparted in the schools, which remained unconnected and, therefore, unapplied in real life situations.[84] It also implied the acceptance of the transformative role of education for the larger society. However, despite this recognition, the action programmes following each such recommendation did not provide any blueprint for such a change. School education is still patterned in such a way that it maintains a very weak position of the teacher; continues to appreciate disjunction between the school and the cultural milieu of the child; and does not attempt to enlist the cooperation of the outside community as a pedagogic resource in the learning process of students.

Given the aforesaid scenario, it becomes an essential political and pedagogic requirement to ensure systematic interaction between schools and the cultural milieu of learners; between "official knowledge" and other forms of knowledges; and between the state and community. In opposition to the present paradigm of schooling—a one way traffic—where outside influences affect the nature of classroom transactions, but the school does not consciously move out of its physical confines to interact with such influences, and where exists a kind of disjunction between the lessons taught in school and outside reality, this paper advocates a different vision of education. This is a vision of pluralism and transformative education, where the school would consciously interact with the community and intervene through its pedagogy in the affairs of the latter and in the process both will be transformed.

It is not a programme of sacrificing the liberal constitutional values mainstream schools stand for. It also does not seek to allow the withdrawal of the state from its educational responsibilities. On the contrary, schools are envisaged in this vision as the agents for the dissemination of progressive values. However, in order to achieve this objective, they should work with and utilise potentials of communities without sacrificing its progressive agenda. In fact, it is an effort to pedagogically and politically use children's inquisitive attitude and their cultural milieu, transformative potentials of education, and the agency of teachers in transforming both school and community.

One core supposition of the paper is that the condition of disconnect between children's cultural milieu and the world of school has not served the objective of promoting the scientific temperament and disseminating transformative education, because the essential pedagogic interaction between the two is missing. Moreover, it is also an effort to underline education as something essentially political and social, instead of a neutral phenomenon. Therefore, in this paper, I have attempted to underscore the need to gear education to achieve social transformation, and to recognise and nurture various kinds of identities as something essential for a plural society.

Although, the objective of this paper is not to present a

detailed blueprint of programme or list of measures, still, by way of concluding examples for social science education, one can suggest that for scientific learning of history, we need significant restructuring of the present paradigm of schooling itself. Such a restructuring should include the elimination of the centrality, finality and compulsory nature of prescribed textbooks in the learning process of students and their evaluation. It also requires support, encouragement and freedom to teachers for creativity; constant and effective utilisation of teaching aids; strict adherence to norms regarding prescribed student-teacher ratio; enabling teachers and schools for taking crucial pedagogic/academic decisions; flexibility in curriculum and timetable; and examination reforms.

Unfortunately, the present drive for examination reforms suffers largely from two shortcomings. First, though it has the potential to break the stranglehold of textbook culture, it seriously compromises the quality concerns in education.[85] Second, these reforms are being proposed and implemented without making other required changes (some of which have already been mentioned above) in the system. This allows us to doubt the possibility of this drive for bringing about any fundamental transformation. Even the Right to Education Act (2009) maintains complete silence regarding pedagogic interaction between the school and the outside world and provides very little to enhance the academic autonomy of the teacher.[86]

Besides the above stated measures, schools should maintain a comprehensive diversity index and regularly update it as recommended by the Sachar Committee.[87] Moreover, community visits should be made a regular phenomenon of school education as part of various kinds of learning exercises, surveys and excursions; and experts of various fields in the community should be invited in the school to contribute in the teaching of their respective skills. Schools should use the potentials of celebrating the festivals of all socio-religious communities with the view to acquaint students with cultural diversity and to orient them to think critically and historically about various issues of social history.

Another way in which schools may attempt to bridge the disjunction between classroom and cultural/social milieu of children is by assigning students project works on those themes, which demand from them pedagogic engagement with the outside community as a learning resource; and teachers should inspire and support them to make activist intervention.[88] Students may be guided to engage in certain projects, which put them in a situation of interaction with the members of other socio-religious communities outside the school. Students may choose themes such as the festivals of various socio-religious communities and geographical regions, diverse modes of worship, dress codes, culinary cultures, familial patterns and glottal varieties.

Such explorations may also cover other issues, such as the employment patterns and the distribution of resources; social discrimination against minorities, marginalised castes, women, disabled and poor people; and the environmental degradation. Students may be asked to explore the processes and the patterns of change as well as resistance in these fields in the recent past. They can also be motivated to connect these with the geography and history of the locality in question.

This should create the possibility for students to interact with the members of other socio-religious communities, economic classes, professional and political groups in both the "private" and "public" spheres", which may provide them greater scope for being sensitive about diversity.

Proper arrangements should be made for the presentation of students' project reports in the school. These projects should be evaluated by a committee of teachers. The practice of assigning project work to the students as part of their internal assessment by the teacher has recently begun in some schools. However, unfortunately, it has become a victim of malpractices of copying from the textbooks, or from the special guides prepared and published by those private publishers, whose only objective is to make a profit. There is a need to ensure that instead of simple reproduction of facts from the study material, such project reports should demonstrate students' live pedagogic interaction with—and wherever possible the intervention in—the communities outside the school.

Some of the measures to ensure this honesty could be community visits and writing of reports in the school under the guidance of teachers; and the presentation of reports in the school before a select committee of teachers in the presence of students and community members. However, all this would require introduction of a number of above mentioned concrete reforms in the system of education, in the work conditions of teachers and their training (both pre-service and in-service) and in the attitude of the school towards the community. Otherwise, these would remain only abstract ideals and like most of the national curriculum frameworks and other policy pronouncements would fail to break any new ground.

NOTE: With the purpose of not disclosing the specific/individual identities of students, we have replaced their original names with fictitious ones, though the cultural affinity between the two has been retained.

NOTES

1. E.g., Emile Durkheim, 1985, (also see other essays in this volume); Antonio Gramsci, 1971; S. Bowles and H. Gintis, 1976; P. Bourdieu, and J.C. Passeron, 1977; Basil Bernstein, 1977; Michael W. Apple, 1979; and Paul Willis, 1981.
2. E.g., Krishna Kumar, 1989 and 2001; A.R. Kamat, 1985; and Suma Chitnis, 1981. Also see, Kancha Ilaiah, 1996: Esp. Ch. 5, pp. 71-101.

3. Unlike Saxena's work, which deals with movements in education, my focus in the present essay is on more common and everyday forms of assertions, resistances and interactions, still for some important insights about this argument, See Sadhna Saxena, 2000.
4. Scholars have recognised that education helps "reproduction", stalemate, or homeostasis in social order. For this argument in the Indian context, see Krishna Kumar, 1985 and 1989; Sabyasachi Bhattacharya, 1998 and 2002; and Sabyasachi Bhattacharya, Joseph Bara and Chinna Rao Yagati, 2001. (Especially see the introductory essays in Bhattacharya's volumes for his theoretical position.) Though unlike some early "reproduction" theorists of the West, Bhattacharya does not imply complete success of the processes of "reproduction" in any deterministic fashion, he still underscores the desire of elites to maintain "homeostasis" as a significant element of the sphere of education in both colonial and national contexts.
5. Michael W. Apple, 2000.
6. Ibid. Also see, Michael W. Apple, 2004.
7. Sarojini Vittachi, Neeraj Raghavan with Kiran Raj, 2007. For this point about non-receptive 'mainstream' system, see especially the 'Foreword' by Krishna Kumar and in *passim*.
8. E.g., Paul Willis, 1981.
9. For the arguments proposed in this paper, I have relied on my own experiences and observations as a social science teacher in the two schools of the Directorate of Education in Delhi. After completing a degree course in education from a reputed institution and before joining the present faculty post at Delhi University, I got the opportunity to work in schools as a Social Science teacher for about four years (2003-2007). In the first school of my appointment in South Delhi, (Sarvodaya Vidyalaya), I worked for about two and a half years. Subsequently, I was transferred to a school in North Delhi (Government Boys Senior Secondary School) where I taught for one and a half years. At both schools, I taught the students of 6th to 10th standards. During two academic sessions, however, I also got the opportunity of teaching the students of 11th and 12th grades when a senior teacher of history in the Sarvodaya Vidyalaya went on long leave.

10. One recent example is Prof. Habib's critique of the National Curriculum Framework (2005). See, Irfan Habib, 2005.
11. See, Footnote Nos. 2, 18 and 37 here.
12. For this assessment, see Francois Leclercq, 2008; Anne Vaugier-Chatterjee, 2004, (especially the essays by Sumit Bose and Anne Vaugier-Chatterjee, Francois Leclercq, Stephane Moulin and Samia Kazi Aoul.) Also see, R. Govinda and Rashmi Diwan, 2003.
13. K.M. Shrimali, 2005.
14. Krishna Kumar's analysis of the school's relations with the child's cultural milieu (though he does not engage with school community interaction as such) may be taken as an example here. See, Krishna Kumar, 2008.
15. I often observed that the classroom discussions of historical characters like Ashoka, Akbar, Mahatma Gandhi and Bhagat Singh, and events such as Partition created opportunities for students to express their views formed by the influence of movies and Television serials.
16. Krishna Kumar, 2008.
17. Ibid.
18. This is evident from various studies on education—including both, classroom experiences and curricular knowledge—exposing its upper caste, middle class, male and 'majoritarian' character. See–Footnote Nos. 1 and 2 above. Also See–Krishna Kumar, 1983.
19. Carlo Ginzburg, 1976 and 1980 (A).
20. Carlo Ginzburg, 1976: p. 35.
21. Cited in Graeme Smith, 2008: pp. 68-9.
22. Graeme Smith, 2008: p. 149.
23. Carlo Ginzburg, 1980 (B): p. XIII.
24. See for example in the Indian context–Partha Chatterjee, 1999: Ch. 4 and 5; Romila Thapar, 1996; and Gyanendra Pandey, 2006: Ch. 4.
25. See for example: 'Rewriting History: A Symposium on Ways of Representing Our Shared Past', *Seminar*, No. 522, (February) 2003: specially the essays by Partha Chatterjee, Tanika Sarkar and Nita Kumar.
26. Various scholars have commented on the question of "objectivism" in history; similarly many historians have critiqued the Foucauldian reduction of history as merely being

fictional. See for example–Jorn Rusen, 1990; Gerard Noiriel, 1994; Sumit Sarkar, 2002: specially Ch. 8; and Aijaz Ahmad, 2000.

27. Roland Barthes, 1975/1993.
28. Hayden White, 1975 and 1984; Roland Barthes 1975/1993; Bernard Dauenhauer, 2005.
29. Hayden White, 1975 and 1984.
30. Eric Hobsbawm, 2000: Esp. Ch. 1, pp. 1-12.
31. E.g., Marc Bloch, 1964; R.G. Collinwood, 1948; and E.H. Carr, 1990.
32. Robert Phillips, 2000.
33. Penelope Harnett, 2000: p. 29 my emphasis.
34. Tony McAleavy, 2000.
35. Here I have relied on Alam Khundmiri's definition of secularism. See, M.T. Ansari, 2001: Esp. Ch. 15, pp. 225-36.
36. For this view of history as the science of the interpretation of traces of past events, see the writings of Paul Ricoeur. For a short reference, see Bernard Dauenhauer, 2005.
37. For the review of earlier NCERT and some provincial textbooks of history, see Krishna Kumar, 2001; and Avijit Pathak, 2002: Esp. Ch. 2. For the controversy on textbooks introduced in the period of the BJP led coalition government at the centre, see *Saffronised and Substandard: A Critique of the New NCERT Textbooks,* SAHMAT, New Delhi, 2002. For the current series of history textbooks of NCERT, see Aditya Sarkar, 2006.
38. Krishna Kumar has traced the origins of this "meek dictatorship" or "weak position" of teachers to the colonial period in the growth of standardized syllabus and textbooks. See, Krishna Kumar, 1991: specially Ch. 4, pp. 71-95; and 1986.
39. Poonam Batra, 2005.
40. However, personally I do not subscribe to the view that the continuance of textbooks is an unavoidable evil for Indian education.
41. The old NCERT textbooks of history were replaced after remaining in use for nearly three decades in 2002. Following this, the SCERT of Delhi decided to introduce its own textbooks, instead of the NCERT textbooks for Classes VI-VIII in 2004, but continued the NCERT textbooks for upper classes. Following another change of regime at the centre,

NCERT once again changed the short-lived textbooks in 2006. Two years ago, the SCERT (Delhi) have withdrawn its textbooks for middle classes and adopted the NCERT textbooks.

42. For detailed reviews of Eklavya's Social Science textbooks, see Poonam Batra, 2010.
43. This is a point on which almost all the National Curriculum frameworks since 1975 have agreed. See–*The Curriculum for The Ten-Year School: A Framework*, NCERT, 1975, (specially Introduction and pp. 22, 29, 34-6 and 53); *National Curriculum for Primary and Secondary Education*, NCERT, 1985, (pp. 18 and 21); *National Curriculum for Elementary and Secondary Education: A Framework, (Revised version)*, NCERT, 1988, (p. 26); and *National Curriculum Framework*, NCERT, 2005, (specially Ch. 2). Also see, the Report of the National Commission for Teachers (1) under the chairmanship of Prof. Chatopadhyaya, Government of India, 1984, pp. 14-5 and 22. It can also be seen in other policy documents, such as the National Policy on Education (NPE), 1968 and NPE, 1986, etc.
44. William Stow and Terry Haydn, 2000.
45. Ibid.
46. Ibid.
47. E.g., in the Indian context, relying on "The general theory of cognitive development, particularly in its Piagetian formulation", this has been advocated by Professor Krishna Kumar. See, Krishna Kumar, 1996: Ch. 2, pp. 25-41.
48. William Stow and Terry Haydn, 2000.
49. See the letter of Prof. Yashpal to the then Human Resource Development Minister Shri Arjun Singh, dated July 15, 1993; and Sadhna Saxena, 2000, (specially Ch. 1, pp. 19-34). Also see the following (cited in Saxena, 2000), R. Govinda and N.V. Vargis, 1993, p. 16; R. Govinda, 1995, p. 33; and Report of the World Bank on Primary Education: Achievements and Challenges, 1996. The reports of Pratham on this subject also focus on very low levels of attainment by the students.
50. For this, see Load of School Bag: Learning Without Burden (Report of the National Advisory Committee) Under the Chairmanship of Prof. Yashpal, constituted by the Ministry of Human Resource and Development, Government of India, 1993.

51. On receipt of the Yashpal Committee's report, a Group was set up on August 25, 1993 under the chairmanship of Shri Y.N. Chaturvedi, Additional Secretary, Department of Education of MHRD. Its purpose was to examine the feasibility of implementing the recommendations made in the report of the Yashpal Committee. The Group submitted its report on October 5, 1993, wherein it suggested that "while there may be some flaws in the syllabi and the textbooks prepared by the NCERT, it does not seem that they can be accused of being grossly unsuitable or overloaded". URL: http://www.education.nic.in/cd50years/home.htm
52. Amartya Sen, 2005: pp. 317-33.
53. For different notions of time and imagination in history, see Romila Thapar, 1996; E.P. Thompson, 1967; Sumit Sarkar, 1997: Ch. 6, pp. 186-215; Dipesh Chakrabarty, 2000; and Prathama Banerjee, 2005. (Also see p. 81 in Banerjee for some useful references on time and imagination.)
54. *Bharat ka Itihas* (Bhaag 2), *for Class 7th*, SCERT, Delhi, Ch. 3, pp. 19-26. (specially pp. 20-1. Also see, Ch. 5, pp. 37-45 specially pp. 42-3.)
55. Tripta Wahi, 2010.
56. For some understanding of the relationship of classroom hierarchy with outside society, see, Talcott Parsons, 'The School Class as a Social System', in Suresh Chandra Shukla and Krishna Kumar (Ed.), 1985.
57. For a brief discussion and relevant references on multiple identities, see various articles as well as the Bibliography in 'A Symposium on the Definitions of the Self', *Seminar*, No. 387, November 1991. Also see, Noonan Harold, 2006.
58. We were reading *Bharat ka Itihas* (*Bhaag 1*), for Class 6th, SCERT, Delhi, 2004, Ch. 12, pp. 108-15, specially *'Dharmon ke Vistar ke Vishay mein aur Jankari 2'*, pp. 114-5.
59. One student had referred to the practice of meat eating amongst Muslims by reading out a sentence from the history textbook for his class published from a private publisher.
60. It is also seen as a tenet of "Sanskritization" amongst the so-called lower castes in the process of seeking upward mobility. See M.N. Srinivas, 1994.
61. For some other preliminary reflections on the perceptions of non-Muslim classmates and teachers about Muslims and their

impact on the Muslim students, see Azra Razzack, 1991.

62. See Michael W. Apple, 1979 and Krishna Kumar, 1996.
63. *Bharat ka Itihas* (*Bhaag* 2), for Class 7th, SCERT, Delhi, 2004, Ch. 11, pp. 96-104.
64. E.g., Makkhan Lal, 2002; and Meenakshi Jain, 2002.
65. *Bharat ka Itihas* (*Bhaag* 2), for Class 7th, SCERT, Delhi, 2004, Ch. 11, specially pp. 97-8.
66. I am thankful to Naresh Kumar for sharing with me his knowledge of the Sikh tradition.
67. William Stow and Terry Haydn, 2000.
68. The debate on Indian secularism has been compiled by Rajeev Bhargava. See, Rajeev Bhargava, 1998.
69. For this argument, see Peter van der Veer and Hartmut Lehmann, 1999: pp. 15-43.
70. M.T. Ansari, (Ed.), 2001: Ch. 15, pp. 225-36.
71. Talal Asad, 1999.
72. *Civics: Part II, Class 10,* NCERT, 2003, Volume 1, Lesson 2, pp. 24-49.
73. In the academic session 2009-2010, there were total 1262526 students—632290 boys (50.09%) +630236 girls (49.91%) — enrolled in all the schools of the Directorate of Education (Delhi) in various classes. Out of which, 175867(13.92%) are SCs, 3229 (0.25%) STs, 26353 (2.08%) OBCs and 170640 (13.51%) are Muslims. Source: This data is based on the response received from the District PIOs on the RTI Applications of Vikas Gupta dated September 3, 2009, ID No. 5250; and Yamal Gupta, dated September 3, 2009, ID No. 5249 in the Directorate of Education.
74. Sacred thread worn by the so-called upper or twice born castes.
75. Students very frequently transgressed the chronological boundaries. Once we were discussing the issue of caste inequalities in context of the ancient period of Indian history in the sixth class. One Dalit student named Arti suddenly began talking about B.R. Ambedkar. Later, she revealed that it was her father who discussed Ambedkar with the family members.
76. The concept of "framing" was originally discussed by Basil Bernstein; and in the Indian context, Padma Sarangapani has used it in her work on a primary school in a village of Delhi.

See, Padma M. Sarangapani, 2003: specially Ch. 6, pp. 124-63.

77. Rabindra Menon, 1959: p. I.
78. Ibid., p. 2.
79. Ibid., p. 5.
80. Ibid., pp. 10-11.
81. Ibid., p. 14.
82. Ibid., p. 20.
83. For an understanding of the ways in which schools become the instrument of silencing and the importance of dialogue in the learning process, see Paulo Freire, 1970: specially Ch. 2. Also see, Paulo Freire, 1998.
84. See footnote No. 47 above.
85. E.g., Teachers' Manual on School Based Assessment: Class IX & X, Central Board of Secondary Education, Delhi, 2009; and The Right of Children for Free and Compulsory Education Act, Government of India, 2009, (Ch. IV, Section 16 and Ch. V, Section 30). Also see other related circulars of CBSE and Directorate of Education (Delhi) regarding "Continuous and Comprehensive Evaluation" of students.
86. The Right of Children for Free and Compulsory Education Act, Government of India, 2009, (specially Ch. V, Section 29).
87. Report on the Social, Economic and Educational Status of the Muslim Community in the Country, submitted by the Committee constituted by the Union Government under the Chairmanship of Justice Rajindar Sachar, 2006.
88. Various interesting examples of this kind have been documented by Michael Apple and James Beane in the US context. Not only some institutions offering alternative education, even some 'mainstream' schools, for example, in Lucknow have been doing such works very effectively in India as well. See–Michael W. Apple and James A. Beane (Ed.), 1999; and 'Students Give Lessons in Social Studies', http://epaper.timesofindia.com/Default/Scripting/ArticleWin.asp?From=Archive&Source=Page&Skin=TOINEW&BaseHref=TOIL/2010/05/14&PageLabel=25&EntityId=Ar02400&ViewMode=HTML&GZ=T' in Cetina K. Knorr and A.V. Cicourel (eds) *Advances in Social Theory and Methodology*, p. 306.

BIBLIOGRAPHY

Reports, Policies and Letters

Letter of Prof. Yashpal to the then Human Resource Development Minister Shri Arjun Singh, dated July 15, 1993 URL: http://www.education.nic.in/cd50years/home.htm

Load of School Bag: Learning Without Burden (Report of the National Advisory Committee) Under the Chairmanship of Prof. Yashpal, constituted by the Ministry of Human Resource and Development, Government of India, 1993.

National Curriculum for Primary and Secondary Education, NCERT, 1985.

National Curriculum for Elementary and Secondary Education: A Framework, (*Revised version*), NCERT, 1988.

National Curriculum Framework, NCERT, 2005.

National Policy on Education, Government of India, 1968.

National Policy on Education, Government of India, 1986 .

Report of the National Commission for Teachers (1) under the chairmanship of Prof. Chatopadhyaya, Government of India, 1984.

Report of the World Bank on Primary Education: Achievements and Challenges, 1996.

Report of the Group under the chairmanship of Shri Y.N. Chaturvedi, Additional Secretary, Department of Education of MHRD to examine the feasibility of implementing the recommendations made in the report of Yashpal Committee, dated October 5,1993. Summary available at URL: http://www.education.nic.in/cd50years/home.htm

RTI Response from the District PIOs on the Application of Vikas Gupta dated September 3, 2009, ID No. 5250 Filed in the Directorate of Education.

RTI Response from the District PIOs on the Application of Yamal Gupta, dated September 3, 2009, ID No. 5249 Filed in the Directorate of Education.

Teachers' Manual on School Based Assessment: Class IX and X, Central Board of Secondary Education, Delhi, 2009.

The Curriculum for the Ten-Year School: A Framework, NCERT, 1975.

The Right of Children for Free and Compulsory Education Act, Government of India, 2009.

Monographs and Articles

A Symposium on the Definitions of the Self, *Seminar*, No. 387, November, 1991.

Ahmad, Aijaz, (2000), 'Postmodernism in History', in K.N. Panikkar and Terence J. Byres Ed., *The Making of History: Essays Presented to Irfan Habib*, Tulika, New Delhi, pp. 440-77.

Ansari, M.T., Ed., (2001), *Secularism, Islam and Modernity: Selected Essays of Alam Khundmiri*, Sage Publications, New Delhi.

Apple, Michael W., (1979), *Ideology and Curriculum*, Routledge and Kegan Paul, London.

(2000), *Official Knowledge: Democratic Education in a Conservative Age*, (Second Edition), Routledge, New York.

(2004), 'Cultural Politics and the Text', In Stephen J. Ball, Ed., *Reader in Sociology of Education*, Routledge Falmer, pp. 179-95.

Apple, Michael W. and Beane, James A., Ed., (1999), *Democratic Schools: Lessons from the Chalk Face*, Open University Press, Buckingham.

Asad, Talal, (1999), 'Religion, Nation-State, Secularism', in Peter van der Veer and Hartmut Lehmann, Ed., *Nation and Religion: Perspectives on Europe and Asia*, Princeton University Press, pp. 178-96.

Banerjee, Prathama, (2005), 'The Work of Imagination: Temporality and Nationhood in Colonial Bengal', in Shahid Amin et al. Ed., *Subaltern Studies*, Vol. 12, Permanent Black, Delhi, pp. 280-322.

Barthes, Roland, (1975), 'An Introduction to the Structural Analysis of Narrative', *New Literary History*, Vol. 6, No. 2. pp. 237-72. Reprinted in Roland Barthes, (1979/1993), *Image-Music-Text*, Fontana Press, Glasgow.

Batra, Poonam, (2005), 'Voice and Agency of Teachers: Missing Link in the National Curriculum Framework 2005', *Economic and Political Weekly (EPW)*, Vol. 40, No. 40, pp. 4347-56.

(2010), Ed., *Social Science Learning in the Schools: Perspectives and Challenges*, Sage Publications, New Delhi.

Bernstein, Basil, (1977), *Class, Codes and Control*, Routledge and Kegan Paul, London.

Bharat ka Itihas (*Bhaag 1*), for sixth class, SCERT, Delhi, 2004.

Bharat ka Itihas (*Bhaag 2*), for seventh class, SCERT, Delhi, 2004.

Bhargava, Rajeev, Ed., (1998), *Secularism and Its Critics*, Oxford University Press.

Bhattacharya, Sabyasachi, Ed., (1998), *The Contested Terrain: Perspectives on Education in India*, Orient Longman Limited.

(2002), *Education and the Disprivileged: Nineteenth and Twentieth Century India*, Orient Longman Private Limited.

Bhattacharya, Sabyasachi, Bara, Joseph and Yagati, Chinna Rao, Ed., (2001), *Development of Women's Education in India: A Collection of Documents (From 1850 to 1920)*, Kanishka, New Delhi.

Bloch, Marc, (1964), *The Historian's Craft*, Vintage.

Bourdieu, P. and Passeron, J.C., (1977), *Reproduction in Education Society and Culture*, Sage Publications, London.

Bowles, S. and Gintis, H., (1976), *Schooling in Capitalist America*, Routledge and Kegan Paul, London.

Carr, E.H., (1990), *What is History?*, Penguin Books.

Chakrabarty, Dipesh, (2000), *Provincializing Europe: Postcolonial Thought and Historical Difference*, Princeton University Press, Princeton.

Chatterjee, Partha, (1999), *Nation and Its Fragments: Colonial and Post-Colonial Histories*, in the Partha Chatterjee Omnibus, Oxford University Press, New Delhi.

Chitnis, Suma, (1981), *A Long Way to Go: Report on a Survey of Scheduled Caste High School and College Students in Fifteen States of India*, Allied Publishers, New Delhi.

Civics: Part II, class 10, NCERT, 2003.

Collingwood, R.G., (1948), *The Idea of History*, Clarendon Press.

Dauenhauer, Bernard, (2005), 'Paul Ricoeur', in Edward N. Zalta (ed.), *The Stanford Encyclopedia of Philosophy*, (Winter). URL = <http://plato.stanford.edu/archives/win2005/entries/ricoeur/>.

Durkheim, Emile, (1985), 'Education: Its Nature and its Role', in Suresh Chandra Shukla and Krishna Kumar Ed., *Sociological Perspectives in Education: A Reader*, Chanakya Publications, Delhi, pp. 9-22.

Freire, Paulo, (1970), *Pedagogy of the Oppressed*, Continuum Publishing Company.

(1998), *Pedagogy of Freedom*, Rowman and Littlefield Publishers.

Ginzburg, Carlo, (1976), 'High and Low: The Theme of Forbidden Knowledge in the Sixteenth and Seventeenth Centuries', *Past and Present*, No. 73, November, pp. 28-41.

(1980 A), 'Morelli, Freud and Sherlock Holmes: Clues and Scientific Method', *History Workshop*, No. 9, (Spring), pp. 5-36.

(1980 B), *The Cheese and the Worms: The Cosmos of a Sixteenth-Century Miller* (First Italian Edition 1976), Translated in English by John and Anne Tedeschi, Routledge and Kegan Paul, London.

Govinda R., (1995), State of Primary Education of the Urban Poor in India, Research Report, No. 5, Paris, UNESCO, IIEP.

Govinda, R. and Diwan, Rashmi, Ed. (2003), *Community Participation and Empowerment in Elementary Education*, Sage Publications, New Delhi.

Govinda, R. and Vargis, N.V., (1993), *Quality of Primary Schooling in India: A Case Study of Madhya Pradesh*, Monograph, New Delhi, NIEPA.

Gramsci, Antonio, (1971), 'On Education', in his *Selections from the Prison Notebooks*, (Translated and Edited by Q. Hoare and G.N. Smith), International Publishers, New York, pp 24-43. URL = <http://www.marxists.org/archive/gramsci/index.htm.

Habib, Irfan, (2005), 'How to Evade Real Issues and Make Room for Obscurantism', *Social Scientist*, Vol. 33, No. 9/10, (Special Issue on Debating Education), pp. 3-12.

Harnett, Penelope, (2000), 'Curriculum Decision-making in the Primary School: The Place of History', in James Arthur and Robert Phillips Ed., *Issues in History Teaching*, Routledge, London, pp. 24-38.

Harold, Noonan, (2006), 'Identity', in Edward N. Zalta Ed., *The Stanford Encyclopedia of Philosophy*, (Winter), URL = <http://plato.stanford.edu/archives/win2006/entries/identity/>.

Hobsbawm, Eric, (2000), *On History*, Abacus.

Ilaiah, Kancha, (1996), *Why I Am Not a Hindu: A Sudra Critique of Hindutva Philosophy, Culture and Political Economy*, Samya.

Jain, Meenakshi, (2002), *Medieval India: A Textbook for class XII*, NCERT.

Kamat, A.R., (1985), *Education and Social Change in India*, Somaiya Publications, Bombay.

Kumar, Krishna, (1983), 'Educational Experience of Scheduled Castes and Tribes', *EPW*, Vol. 18, No. 36, pp. 1566-72.

(1985), 'Reproduction or Change? Education and Elites in India', *EPW*, Vol XX, No. 30, pp. 1280-84.

(1986), 'Textbooks and Educational Culture', *EPW*, Vol. 21, No. 30, pp. 1309-11.

(1989), *Social Character of Learning*, Sage Publications, New Delhi.

(1991), *Political Agenda of Education: A Study of Colonialist and Nationalist Ideas*, Sage Publications, New Delhi.

(1996), *Learning from Conflict*, Orient Longman, New Delhi.

(2001), *Prejudice and Pride: School Histories of the Freedom Struggle in India and Pakistan*, Penguin Books, New Delhi.

(2008), 'Education and Culture: India's Quest for a Secular Policy', in Krishna Kumar and Joachim Oesterheld Ed., *Education and Social Change in South Asia*, Orient Longman, New Delhi, pp. 196-217.

Lal, Makkhan, (2002), *Ancient India: A Textbook for Class XI*, NCERT.

Leclercq, Francois, (2008), 'Decentralisation of School Management and Quality of Teaching', in Krishna Kumar and Joachim Oesterheld, Ed., *Education and Social Change in South Asia*, Orient Longman, New Delhi, pp. 475-505.

McAleavy, Tony, (2000, 'Teaching About Interpretations', in James Arthur and Robert Phillips, Ed), *Issues in History Teaching*, Routledge, London, pp. 72-82.

Menon, Rabindra, (1959), *The Teacher and the Parent*, Ministry of Education (Government of India), Publication No. 421.

Noiriel, Gerard, (1994), 'Foucault and History: The Lessons of a Disillusion', *The Journal of Modern History*, Vol. 66, No. 3, September, pp. 547-68.

Pandey, Gyanendra, (2006), *The Construction of Communalism in Colonial North India*, (Second Edition), Oxford University Press.

Parsons, Talcott, (1985), 'The School Class as a Social System', in Suresh Chandra Shukla and Krishna Kumar, Ed., *Sociological Perspectives in Education: A Reader*, Chanakya Publications, Delhi, pp. 50-75.

Pathak, Avijit, (2002), *Social Implications of Schooling: Knowledge, Pedagogy and Consciousness*, Rainbow Publishers, Delhi.

Phillips, Robert, (2000), 'Government Policies, the State and the Teaching of History', in James Arthur and Robert Phillips, Ed., *Issues in History Teaching*, Routledge, London, pp. 10-23.

Razzack, Azra, (1991), 'Growing up Muslim', *Seminar*, No. 387, pp. 30-3.

Rewriting History: A Symposium on Ways of Representing Our Shared Past, *Seminar*, No. 522, February 2003.

Rusen, Jorn, (1990), 'Rhetoric and Aesthetics of History: Leopold von Ranke', *History and Theory*, Vol. 29, No. 2, (May), pp. 190-204.

Saffronised and Substandard: A Critique of the New NCERT Textbooks, SAHMAT, New Delhi, 2002.

Sarangapani, Padma M., (2003), *Constructing School Knowledge: An Ethnography of Learning in an Indian Village*, Sage Publications.

Sarkar, Aditya, (2006), 'History Textbooks', (Review Article), *Contemporary Education Dialogue*, Vol. 4, No. 1, (Monsoon), pp. 163-71.

Sarkar, Sumit, (1997), *Writing Social History*, Oxford University Press, New Delhi.

(2002), *Beyond Nationalist Frames: Relocating Postmodernism, Hindutva, History*, Permanent Black, New Delhi.

Saxena, Sadhna, (2000), *Shiksha aur Jan Andolan*, Granth Shilpi, Delhi.

Sen, Amartya, (2005), *The Argumentative Indian: Writings on Indian History, Culture and Identity*, Allen Lane (Penguin Books Ltd), London.

Shrimali, K.M., (2005), 'Another Retreat of Reason', *Social Scientist*, Vol. 33, No. 9/10, Debating Education (September - October), pp. 41-6.

Smith, Graeme, (2008), *A Short History of Secularism*, I.B. Tauris Co Ltd, London.

Srinivas, M.N., (1994), *Dominant Caste and Other Essays*, Oxford University Press.

Stow, William, and Haydn Terry, (2000), 'Issues in the Teaching of Chronology', in James Arthur and Robert Phillips, Ed., *Issues in History Teaching*, Routledge, London, pp. 83-97.

Thapar, Romila, (1996), *Time as a Metaphor of History*, Oxford University Press, USA.

Thompson, E.P., (1967), 'Time, Work, Discipline and Industrial Capitalism', *Past and Present*, No. 38, (December), pp. 56-97.

van der Veer, Peter, and Lehmann, Hartmut, (1999), Ed., *Nation and Religion: Perspectives on Europe and Asia*, Princeton University Press.

Vaugier-Chatterjee, Anne, (2004), Ed., *Education and Democracy in India*, Manohar, New Delhi.

Vittachi, Sarojini, Raghavan, Neeraj, with Raj, Kiran, (2007), Ed., *Alternative Schooling in India*, Sage Publications, Delhi.

Wahi, Tripta, (2010), 'History Curriculum and the Textbooks', in Poonam Batra, Ed., *Social Science Learning in the Schools: Perspectives and Challenges*, Sage Publications, New Delhi, pp. 155-96.

White, Hayden, (1975), *Metahistory: The Historical Imagination in Nineteenth-Century Europe*, Johns Hopkins University Press, Baltimore.

(1984), 'The Question of Narrative in Contemporary Historical Theory', *History and Theory*, Vol. 23, No. 1. (February), pp. 1-33.

Willis, Paul, (1981), *Learning to Labor: How Working Class Kids Get Working Class Jobs*, Columbia University Press, New York.

2

Understanding Scientific History

Mahima Singh

It is somewhat fashionable to emphasise the need to adopt a "scientific" approach to writing history. The very word "scientific", besides adding to academic fashionability, by virtue of its usage also seems to imply an understood credibility to an argument. Keeping this in mind, the attempt of this paper is to build a historical as well as a practical understanding of the phrase "scientific history". To this effect, it is important to state that while there have been several claimants to "scientific history" (self-proclaimed or otherwise), the claims as such have been made based on placing history and natural sciences on the same platform not only in terms of methodology adopted in constructing the body of knowledge under the two disciplines, but also to the very nature of the knowledge produced. In the course of this paper, I would like then to present a brief historiographical background to the 19th century "scientific history" albeit only in the Western historiographical tradition, moving to a brief discussion of an understanding of the method of science as applied to historical construction, drawing largely from the writings of E.H. Carr, and concluding with a somewhat functional understanding of "scientific history".

I

The earliest claims to the scientific status of history coincided with the professionalisation of the discipline in Western scholarship by the mid 19th century.[1] As Iggers states, within the contemporary philosophical milieu 'historians shared the optimism of the professionalised sciences generally that methodologically controlled research makes objective knowledge possible.'[2] This statement enunciates two aspects of contemporary historical scholarship — the employment of methods of science in historical reconstruction and the conception that there indeed was an objective historical reality that could be reconstructed. Eckhardt Fusch broadly differentiates between two trends in what he calls the "historical science" scholarship of the 19th century — first, inspired by German idealist philosophy that focused on the "science of history" which emphasised event-oriented (primarily political) history and upon individual personalities, identified with historicism[3]; second, those who adopted the nomothetic, positivistic methodology employed by contemporary natural sciences, to propound historical laws.[4] At centre stage of the former was Leopold von Ranke whose methodology was conceptualised in historicism (that humans were products of contemporary circumstances, and that everything human had its own structure and development) and the critical perusal of primary, particularly archival sources which could perhaps be considered the cornerstone of the scientificity of his method. History could not be understood by putting forth general assessments of predetermined ideas and values, but by understanding the object's individual history. Ranke's argument was that, in Iggers' words, 'history chose to acquire an understanding of the general through the immersion in the particular. ... While Ranke stressed the necessity of proceeding from critical reconstruction of the events which constitute history, he was also convinced that out of this reconstruction of the past, ["as it actually was"] great forces which shaped history would become apparent. ... The purpose of historical study was therefore not exhausted by the narrative reconstruction of a factual past but consisted in grasping the overarching coherence into which this past fit.'[5] For an analysis of the second category of "scientific historians", Fuchs highlights Comte's contribution to building bridges between methodology implied in natural and social sciences. With the impetus of positivism, laws of history could be drafted to give causal explanations to human behaviour. Here Fuchs cites the critical work of English historian Henry Thomas Buckle whose conception of "scientific history" was different from the German historicists. Fuchs says, ' ... for Buckle the history of mankind was based on historical laws that can be found and explained by historians through the application of "scientific methods," such as statistics, and through the use of the latest findings of the natural sciences, such as meteorological, geological, and psychological knowledge. History was to be made "scientific" on the model of the explanatory character of the natural sciences.'[6] Having enunciated this difference in the two approaches, Fuchs, at the same time, argues that "science of history" and "scientific history" should not be seen as mutually exclusive approaches to "historical science" in general as both held objectivism and seeking universal truth as their core tenets, yet adopted a teleological view of history. He also goes on to say that the process of "scientification of history" was largely influenced by both nationalism as well as Eurocentricism – 'A main social and political purpose of historiography was to offer general social norms and scientifically authenticated and authorised historical model in order to create a national myth that places one's own nation at the center of historical discourse. Aimed at legitimising political and cultural values, history was instrumentalised for national purposes.'[7] Herein lies the irony of the "historical science" discourse of the 19th century; while today one would commonly consider anything "scientific" to be as far removed from subjectivity as possible, bereft of emotional leanings, the very discourse that gave the word "scientific" an etymological grounding in the first place betrayed itself by becoming victim to its own historical context, proving its own tenets inevitably fallible. This in no manner implies that the 19th century discourse around "historical science" should be considered next to redundant in trying to understand what "scientific history" could mean for us at present; undoubtedly this historiography only enriches our understanding of the meaning we ascribe to the term. But at the same time it would perhaps do us best to embrace the fragility of such theoretical constructs when employed with pragmatic injudiciousness across varying temporal contexts.

The turn of the century witnessed what could be called the social science challenge to German "scientific history" which, as part of the scientific method, emphasised theory around human action. The response of social sciences took serious objection to older historiography's exclusive focus on individuals and political events. Iggers aptly writes, '... social science approaches whether Marxist, Parsonian, or Annalist, represented a democratisation of history, an inclusion of broader segments of the population, and an extension of the historical perspective from politics to society. They objected to the older approaches, not because they were scientific but because they were not sufficiently so. They challenged one of the basic assumptions of this older approach, namely that history deals with particulars, not generalisations, that its aim is to "understand," not to "explain," and they maintained instead that all sciences, including history, must include causal explanations.'[8] This is not to say that there were no remnants from the older historiographical tradition into the evolving social science approach; central to the social science approach was the belief in a linear conception of time, the evolution of society in a particular, definitive direction, a conception that subtly entailed the idea of one, evolving history. Also, though this approach to researching human society was no doubt modelled more closely after researches in natural sciences, focusing on social structure and process of social change, it still catered to the concept of there being an objective reality of human past.

It is also interesting that this approach was broadly marked with the supplementation of narrative writing with analytical, thematic or "structural" discourse within the historical literary tradition. Conceptual clarity on the method of historical conjecture has also been provided by discourse on the nature of historical literary tradition.[9] In Lawrence Stone's understanding, 20th century historiography was widely influenced by both Marxist and social science methodology in general, and aimed at producing "scientific history" to explain historical development through theorising general laws around human behaviour. Beginning with Ranke's conceptions of history which Stone calls 'the first "scientific history,"'[10] Stone put forth three significant trends from the 1930s to the 1970s in the production of "scientific history" which upheld different methodologies — the Marxist model based on historical materialism which rested on simplistic economic or social determinism; the French Annalists that laid pivotal importance upon the relationship between food supply and demography; and the American "cleometricians" who he brutally called 'statistical junkies'[11] who were economic and demographic historians basing their researches almost entirely on quantitative data. These histories were characterised by a confidence in being able to ascertain scientific explanations for historical change and human condition based on scientific methodology. However, Stone argues, several historians diagnosed a deficiency in the analytical and structural approaches to history by the proponents of "scientific history" as they relegated the realm of intellectual, religious and cultural ideas to an inconspicuous and insignificant background. In formulating this logic of transformation of the historical literary tradition, Stone makes a simple yet elegant appeal for a rich and holistic historical analysis: 'The historical record has now obliged many of us to admit that there is an extraordinarily complex two-way flow of interactions between facts of population, food supply, climate, bullion supply, prices, on the one hand, and values, ideas and custom on the other. Along with social relationships of status or class, they form a single web of meaning.'[12] Stone, to emphasize the point that ideas are 'potentially at least as important causal agents of change as the impersonal forces of material output and demographic growth'[13], refers to Michael Zuckerman's 'Dream That Men Dare to Dream: The Role of Ideas in Western Modernisation'[14] in which Zuckerman states, 'If we would come to any comprehension of such times [the time of modernisation], we will have to make our difficult way between easy assumptions of techno-economic determinism and easy assertions of individual freedom. We will have to fathom a collective psychic current – a social character or communal sensibility, or a leading edge of it, at any rate – that is crucial in alterations such as those of early modernisation yet is creative and uncoerced rather than being merely an aspect of cosmic determinism customarily associated with imputations of underlying social forces.'[15] However, Zuckerman admits the fallacy of adopting merely one dimension of explanation: 'Of course, it may still be argued that mentalistic explanations are distinctively disreputable because they are so blatantly tautological, their mentation generally being inferred from socio-cultural phenomena and then used to explain such phenomena ... there is no point in denying such an argument.'[16]

In a similar manner, Peter Burke, makes a plea for the integration of two literary traditions – narrative and structural/analytical – underlying which is the need to 'relate local events more closely to structural changes.'[17] Burke does this by comparing two studies of the mutiny of

1857 – the first, by Christopher Hibbert, *The Great Mutiny*, which gives a detailed, narrative account of the events that took place without accounting for why they did; and the second, by Eric Stokes in his *The Peasant and the Raj* which presents an analysis of the context of the revolts, their geography and sociology. In analogising these two studies, Burke soundly states that a synthesis between the chronicler account and structural investigation would prove to be a more comprehensive study.

II

A seminal work on historiography is E.H. Carr's excellent *What is History?* which lays the theoretical foundation on which any historical construction must stand. In placing both social and physical sciences on the same platform in terms of how they contribute to human understanding, Carr succinctly states: 'Scientists, social scientists, and historians are all engaged in different branches of the same study: the study of man and his environment, of the effects of man on his environment and of his environment on man. The object of the study is the same: to increase man's understanding of, and mastery over, his environment. ... the historian and the physical scientist are united in the fundamental purpose of seeking to explain, and in the fundamental procedure of question and answer.'[18] Having said this, what concerns us for the purpose of this paper is how history draws from the methodology of constructing knowledge employed in natural sciences, and what then can be our conclusion on a "scientific" history. Or, otherwise stated in broader terms, what is the extent to which methods of knowledge generation evolved in the study of natural sciences can be applied to other areas of study, like the study of human relationships and culture?

One could begin with what Clayton Roberts says – ' ... the behaviour of human beings does not exhibit the regularity necessary to establish laws governing their behaviour. People do not always vote according to their economic status in the way that a rock always accelerates towards the ground at thirty-two feet per second per second...the law of uniformity, which allows the scientist to speak of all sulphuric acid or all beetles, does not operate in the sphere of human action. ... Historians are not less profound than scientists; they are simply studying behaviour that exhibits far less regularity.'[19] This is not to say that laws in physical sciences cannot be subject to further investigation in the face of new evidence, but the variables of human behaviour are too numerable to even facilitate the forming of laws. But as Carr states, not only has '[the historian] abandoned the search for basic laws, and is content to inquire how things work,'[20] but that the concept of laws has become 'old-fashioned' and 'presumptuous' to physical scientists and social scientists alike, and that 'laws are statements of tendency ... they do not claim to predict what will happen in concrete cases'.[21] Carr insightfully states, 'It is recognised that scientists make discoveries and acquire fresh knowledge, not by establishing precise and comprehensive laws, but by enunciating hypotheses which open the way to fresh inquiry.'[22] Perhaps then the social scientist adopts the following logic to find out how things work – he/she first formulates concepts around human behaviour, the things that make us tick in a particular direction, on the basis of which he/she postulates an hypothesis around the subject under perusal. In history writing, these concepts are formed by the historian once he/she gets acquainted with the observable data, in this case, the sources of history.

All history is hypothesising and is entirely interpretive. As Geoffrey Barraclough said, history is 'not factual at all, but a series of accepted judgements.'[23] But a major difference between the physical science and history is that in the latter, an hypothesis cannot be tested and, therefore, validated *because the variables in which validation should take place will never be constant* – the crucial variables being space (geography) and more importantly, time, among others. And this is why history can never repeat itself. Since no history can conclude with 'hence proved' like in Boolean algebra, with one definitive explanation for the past, the historian tries to look for consistencies in human thought across time and space to make humankind's evolutionary processes more intelligible. The study of artistic delineations or religion certainly entails looking for patterns of human thought that are customised versions of universal patterns, for example, in understanding the elusive 'mother goddess', or burials, or the depiction of the symbol of the cross – concepts that may have emerged as a result of human interaction with the environment.

'All thinking requires acceptance of certain presuppositions [concepts] based on observation, which make scientific thinking possible but [these presuppositions] are subject to revision in the light of that thinking. These hypotheses may well be valid in some contexts or for some purposes, though they turn out to be invalid in others [because of the variables]. *The test in all cases is the empirical one, whether they are in fact effective in promoting fresh insights and adding to our knowledge.*'[24] The test is not, unlike the physical sciences, the validation of the hypothesis to lead to the construction of a model. Though of course, if one looks at the 'segmentary state model' of Burton Stein or Indian feudalism as a 'model', we are really just looking at unconfirmed hypotheses. Nevertheless we call them models because they are larger frameworks within which historians try to fit other processes.

A crucial aspect that the historian must be conscious of is the element of subjectivity. For Carr, what is peculiar about the social sciences in general is that both object and subject are the same and share an interdependent relationship. The very process of observation modifies the nature of what is being observed. Carr subtly warns the reader of the inevitability of bias and subjectivity when he states: 'Objectivity in history ... cannot be an objectivity of fact, but only of relation, of the relation between fact and interpretation, between past, present and future,' and that history cannot deal with absolutes of any kind[25] He further goes on to say: 'When we call a historian objective, we mean I think two things. First of all, we mean that he has a capacity to rise above the limited version of his own situation in society and in history – a capacity which is ... partly dependent on his capacity to recognise the extent of his own involvement in that situation, to recognise, that is to say, the impossibility of total objectivity. Secondly, we mean that he has the capacity to project his vision into the future is such a way as to give him a more profound and more lasting insight into the past than can be attained by those historians whose outlook is entirely bound by his own immediate situation.'[26] Here I would like to say that Carr's former qualification regarding the historian's sensitivity to his own position when logically extended also brings to light the significance of historiography in history writing. Historiography, which in itself is a metatheory in history writing, takes the variable of the position of the observer into consideration, thus enriching his work. Historiography in general merely takes into account the subjectivity of all those who have written before, a subjectivity that is inescapable even in the physical sciences. In this manner, taking historiography into perusal indeed adds to the scientificity of the historian's method. In his analysis of objectivity (and by extension subjectivity) in history, Carr deeply scrutinised the resemblances between history and the natural sciences in terms of methodology, and, as R.W. Davies states, was impacted by the works of such philosophers of science as Thomas Kuhn who spoke of the relativism of the scientific method.[27] Kuhn spoke of subjectivity in scientific knowledge and method, as both evolve within broader cultural frameworks, that what was scientific a century ago may not be considered so today.[28] Influenced by such an understanding, Carr was vociferous in embracing subjectivity as an indispensable aspect of historical conjecture.

Finally, a note on making generalisations in history. Carr aptly commented on the historian's inductive logic, saying that 'the historian is not really interested in the unique, but in what is general in the unique.'[29] which is also truthful in that history writing is not bereft of generalisations. He boldly went on to say, 'it is nonsense to say that generalisation is foreign to history; history thrives on generalisations.' But in history writing the danger lies in generalisations that could take place at another level – when a hypothesis is built around *acquired* concepts, and not concepts built on a balanced observation of all the available sources. By an "acquired" concept we mean preconceived notions which are often emotionally laden, unsubstantiated by a body of observed data, based on personal biases and agenda. In dealing essentially with the question of identity, history writing has been volatile, often victim to assault. Perhaps it would do us best to acknowledge that every disagreement or polarity of thought is another step towards a fresh understanding and building a wider knowledge base.

III

To my understanding, "scientific history" entails a history that does justice to the variety of sources, be they primary or secondary[30], is sensitive to historical contexts determined not by one concept (for example, historical materialism or idea-based determinism), and accepts that human beings are complex enough for no one aspect to determine their behaviour in entirety. In this way, being "scientific" might imply an attempt to develop concepts (generic or contextual) around the *why* of human behaviour by the analysis of sources, and in turn analysing sources by applying these concepts[31], and then building a hypothesis. Uni-dimensional determinism has no scope in any history that claims itself to be "scientific".

I would also like to add that perhaps being "scientific" in history has a simpler, less academic meaning – being open-minded and objective about subjectivity. In this way, being "scientific" in history writing would acknowledge a colloquial understanding of scientificity, i.e. giving convincing reasons behind why we study something the way we study it. It is perhaps because natural/physical sciences have been put on the pedestal of being part of that knowledge closest to an objective reality that academics dealing with human behaviour have felt compelled to equate themselves with sciences altogether, to feel that what they are contributing to is indeed legitimate knowledge. Such an inferiority complex would in part also explain why we have chosen to discuss "scientific history" at all, otherwise this symposium might simply have been on the nature and method of historical reconstruction. Does it imply that studies around human behaviour, be they of the past or present, must be taken seriously provided they validate themselves to be "scientific" in whatever way? That I leave for the reader to think about.

Studies around human behaviour need simply be open to embracing the diversity of human experience, material and mental, in varying contexts at varying points in time, so that they are sensitive to the diversity and capacity of human thought which indeed drives the experience. Once any study is sensitive to this, it can neither be simplistically narrative, nor deterministic, nor jingoistic.

NOTES

1. Iggers, Georg G., *Historiography in the Twentieth Century*, Weslyan University Press, Connecticut, 1997.
2. Ibid., p. 2.
3. For 'historicism', see Georg G. Iggers 'Historicism: The History and Meaning of the Term', *Journal of the History of Ideas*, Vol. 56, No. 1 (January, 1995), pp. 129-52.
4. Fuchs, Eckhardt, 'Conceptions of Scientific History in the

Nineteenth-Century West', in Q. Edward Wang and Georg G. Iggers (eds) *Turning Points in Historiography: A Cross-Cultural Perspective*, University of Rochester Press, 2002. However, Fuchs states that "historical science" scholarship was not exclusively confined to the two mentioned approaches, and that 'although German professional institutions and the idea of "science of history" were adopted by other countries, they were modified to allow variations and alternative approaches.' (p. 149)

5. Iggers, 1995, op. cit., p. 131. In another article Iggers throws light upon the conceptions around Ranke as being a key proponent of "scientific history" not only in European (particularly German) but American historical scholarship as well: 'Unable to understand the philosophic context of Ranke's historical thought, American historians detached Ranke's critical analysis of documents, which they understood and which suited their need to give to history scientific respectability, from his idealistic philosophy, which was alien to them. They transplanted the critical method and seminar into the intellectual setting of the late 19th century America. Ranke thus came to be viewed by almost all historians in the United States ... as the father of "scientific" history, as a non-philosophical historian concerned with the establishment of facts, particularly in the political and institutional realms.' ('The Image of Ranke in American and German Historical Thought', *History and Theory*, Vol. 2, No. 1, 1962, p. 18) Perhaps at an informal, non-academic level, such an image of Ranke persists into the present day.
6. Fuchs, op. cit., p. 150. Romila Thapar, too, makes brief mention of Auguste Comte's contribution to the historiography of ancient India in 'Interpretations of Ancient Indian History', *History and Theory*, Vol. 7, No. 3 (1968), pp. 318-335. Thapar contrasts the works of German and French writers with those of British scholars, as writings of the latter were undoubtedly influenced by colonial agenda and duty. In assessing positivism's impact on ancient Indian historiography she states, 'The keynote to [French and German writers'] understanding was struck by Auguste Comte, who was generally sympathetic to the early Indian tradition, partly due to the influence of the Orientalists but also due to the interest

of French and German sociological thought in the nature of industrialization and its relation to social organisation.' (p. 324) Thapar goes on to state that it was within such a tradition of scholarship that works such as Louis Dumont's *Homo Hierarchicus* can be placed.

7. Fuchs, op. cit., pp. 156-7. This has also been conceded to in Gerog G. Iggers and Harold T. Parker (eds), *International Handbook of Historical Studies: Contemporary Research and Theory*, 1980.
8. Iggers, 1997, op. cit., p. 4.
9. Stone, Lawrence, 'The Revival of Narrative: Reflection on New Old History', *Past & Present*, No. 85 (November, 1979), pp. 3-24.
10. Ibid., p. 5.
11. Ibid., p. 21.
12. Ibid., p. 8.
13. Ibid., p. 9.
14. In *Social Science History*, Vol. 2, No. 3 (Spring, 1978), pp. 332-45.
15. Ibid., p. 339.
16. Ibid., p. 340.
17. Peter Burke, 'History of Events and the Revival of Narrative' from Geoffrey Roberts (ed) *The Narrative History Reader*, p. 308. Burke also speaks of the ambiguity yet confident polarity of the terms "event" (as a circumstance that was) and "structure" (a concept focusing on patterns of social relationships) in the manner in which they are employed in the narrative and analytic discourses respectively, the usage of which limits room for a concept in the middle that may be characterised by, say, political ideology or even individual psychology.
18. Carr, E.H., *What is History?*, 2nd edn., Penguin Books, London, 1987, p. 86.
19. Roberts, Clayton, *The Logic of Historical Explanation*, The Pennsylvania State University, p. 157.
20. Carr, op. cit., p. 60.
21. Ibid., p. 68.
22. Ibid., p. 59.
23. Cited in ibid., p. 61
24. Ibid., p. 56, emphasis added.
25. Ibid., p. 120.
26. Ibid., p. 123.

27. R.W. Davies, 'From E.H. Carr's Files: Notes towards a Second Edition of *What is History?*', in Ibid., p. 163.
28. Thomas Kuhn, *The Structure of Scientific Revolutions*, 3rd edn, The University of Chicago Press, 1996. The soundness of Kuhn's analysis lay in his understanding of the role of history which needs to 'display the historical integrity of [a particular] science in its own time,' stating that 'out-of-date theories are not unscientific because they have been discarded.' (pp. 2-3).
29. Carr, op. cit., p. 63.
30. Often primary sources are considered the apex of any agreeable piece of work, but one could state that secondary sources are indeed of equal importance as they trigger debate and further research and dialogue, contributing to the richness of the discourse in general. As Carr said, 'hypotheses are indispensable tools of thought.' Carr op. cit ., p. 60.
31. Carr calls this method of science 'reciprocal', ibid., p. 59.

3

History a Science? : Challenges of Communicating Scientific History

Smita Sahgal

Notwithstanding the fact that I have no experience of teaching in a school, I have ventured to make a presentation today primarily because the students I interact with within the college come fresh from school. In a sense, then, I have some idea about their mental makeup and attitude towards the discipline of History. I have been teaching History Honours courses at Delhi University for over two decades. I regard this conference a unique opportunity to share with you all my experiences both as a teacher and a researcher in a long quest to explore historical spaces, evolve pedagogic skills, and hone the knack of comprehension that comes with continuous interaction with young inquisitive minds. At the outset I can state with a degree of certitude that teaching History to undergraduate students is an exercise fraught with challenges and excitement. The task becomes all the more taxing when one declares to the students that the discipline they would study for the next three years is scientific. This often surprises them. They can't figure out the connection between science and history. Young minds, fresh out of school, have formulated their own notions of what science is and in most cases the discipline of history represents the polar opposite of that.

So as a preliminary interactive exercise with the first year History Honours students, I enquire of those students, especially those who have switched from the science stream [frequently they have been forced to do so because of getting unexpectedly low marks], to draw out some vital differences, which in their perception would distinguish science subjects from history. Their immediate response is that science subjects teach them to be *rational* in their approach to any topic of discussion while history hinges on learning by rote. The implication is very clear; history is like 'received wisdom' that has to be absorbed and memorised while science subjects provide the students with an opportunity to participate in the process of arriving at anything that can be construed as truth. 'It is so much more inclusive', I often get a response. 'We study the laws of motion, theories on buoyancy, various theorems that are used in civil engineering and all that seem to be explicable. We are not told that rain is a gift from God; we study the process of evaporation, condensation, and cloud formation and finally the rainfall and if the rain fails, we can trace it to global warming or any such cause'. What we study is *causation* in the natural phenomenon or even a cultured one', students tell me. 'History on the other hand only records what has happened in the past and expect us to reproduce the information verbatim in our exam papers. Where is our participation in developing a fact beyond being a mere onlooker and possibly passing the information on to someone else without verifying it?' I am also informed that History courses are dynasty based; it's enough to know about a few rulers and their battles along with memorising some dates of 'important events' and one can be through with studying the essentials of history. Some students have also told me that history appears to be anecdotal and hence not a serious discipline to pursue. Interestingly, many students who seem to have come to the course out of volition also tell me that it is the story like quality of the discipline that attracted them to it, apart from the fact that it is still among the coveted disciplines for the examination to enter the Civil Services of India.

I

I have confronted, and continue to do, such responses early in the day and brace myself with the daunting task of denting them. I have often been reminded of an old Hindi film song which runs something like this, ' *Sikander ne Porus se ki thi ladai, Jo ki thi ladai to main kya karun*? [I know that Alexander fought a war with King Porus. But why should it matter to me? What am I supposed to do?] The context of the song in the film was a history assignment given to the class of young boys and on the teacher's exit they enquire of each other what were they getting from studying history. I have always nurtured the fear that in my absence, too, students would be wondering if they had made a right choice at this crucial juncture in their lives and career by specialising in History Honours . I can easily figure out that a strong dislike for the course has emanated largely from the way history is being taught at the school level and if it is willingly chosen at the college level it certainly is not for the love of the discipline. I realise that most of the students end up pursuing the History Honours course for the wrong reasons. Over the years, the first few months are spent in the process of unlearning what they have absorbed in the preceding few years and then we all look at the possibility of discovering the scientific dimension of the discipline. The aim is clear: to introduce students to history education that evolves each of them into 'thinking students' who understand the primacy of reason and to make them better citizens.

II

A couple of years ago; with the assistance of some of my students I designed a questionnaire especially for the first year students. This exercise was primarily undertaken to become acquainted with their standing on the subject so that I know where to pitch in my lectures. In the process I also got apprised of the areas that need to be taken up for incisive analysis. Today I am going to use that data to ascertain their levels of curiosity, build some assessments in terms of general perceptions about the discipline and also attempt to challenge a few stereotypes. The sample size in form of the survey undertaken is not too big; just about forty History Honours students have been covered. Hence, I am vulnerable to criticism if I seek to generalise too much, yet years of teaching experience accrued within Delhi University and outside and through numerous syllabus revision exercises do equip me in a certain way to comment on the level of students' perspicacity and areas where they needed guidance to evolve their own arguments.

Some of the queries taken up for analysis [both for class discussions as well as in the questionnaire] included issues such as what constitutes science? What is social science? How central is the study of causation to history? Are historical paradigms as testable as those of traditionally recognised scientific disciplines? Can history be associated with predictive accuracy? Can objective reality be easily accessed or is the past we study only a construct of human minds? A very basic issue enquired was what is a historical fact? Can everything that has happened in the past come within the ambit of a historical fact or is a historical fact something to which historians impute a relevance in the sense that it is debated upon as significant in contributing to human development or is historical fact still constituted of something which the power wielding individuals would want posterity to know? Can myths be taken as pieces of history? If so, how do we distinguish one from another? Are 'historical truths' verifiable? In other words, how empirical is history as a discipline and how objective can one be in historical assessments? Can studying history infuse scientific temper amongst the young generation? I also enquired how relevant is the study of history in the contemporary set up? How does it contribute to a better comprehension of the world around us? On the other hand, can history be abused by those in authority both within society and specifically in politics? There were other issues as well regarding how history should be periodised, what, in their opinion, was the role of chance in history or that of an individual in shaping the course of historical processes.

The responses were varied but on some issues, as cited above, the responses were quick and similar. In a query on charting out differences and commonality between history and science, I was told, that science assumes that the universe is empirical, operates according to law like principles, and human beings can discover those laws and use them rationally. One of the vital 'perceived' differences then was the 'centrality of causation' in science and its absence in a historical discourse. The other aspect was its governance by certain principles that could be repeatedly put to test. The 'truth' that science subjects arrived or attempted to arrive at, my students informed me, was fully substantiated through experiments and could be explained in humanly intelligible format even if it appeared to be quite abstruse. Moreover the continuous human engagement with the science disciplines opened up vistas for further enquiry and added to rich repertoires of knowledge through interactive processes that appear to be conspicuous by their absence in any historical study. By this explanation history certainly seemed to be a dry subject that marginalised logic and did not let the participants arrive at plausible truths through self-engagement with the discipline. They were not aware that a certain methodology is at work and without the application of reason; no tenable historical explanations can be put forth.

I have had to explain it to them that 'causation' is the *raison d'être* of the discipline. History, too, has adopted the scientific method of research. A scientific method of research would seek to explain events of nature in a reproducible way. This is supposed to be done through observation of a natural phenomenon, and or through experimentation that tries to simulate natural events under controlled conditions. Based on observation of a phenomenon, collection of relevant data, a scientist may generate a model or suggest a hypothesis to explain the phenomenon. This description can then be used to make predictions that are testable by experiment or observation using the scientific method. When a hypothesis is proved unsatisfactory, it is either modified or discarded. Within the discipline of history, too, this methodology has been adopted. No historical hypothesis can be constructed without studying the primary sources which too need to be contextualised temporally and spatially. These are our tools for reconstructing our past. The sources could be textual, oral, archaeological, epigraphic or numismatic and a meticulous study of each helps us to reflect on a variety of social dimensions of a historical phase. At times the information gathered could conflict and therefore has to be used very cautiously but there would be occasions that the historical information is verified from different sources and hence becomes more acceptable. With the data at our disposal we begin the process of explaining why such events/ processes took place and then revisit the model constructed to plug gaps. For instance, production of food in prehistory cannot be cited as an organically evolutionary process that would have happened around the world on its own without serious human effort. It came about when humanity suffered acute food shortages with the rise of population and climatic changes and looked for sustainable sources of food in potentially fertile zones. This slow process materialised after years of observation and experimentation but changed the course of history of humanity once it was arrived at. I explain it to my students that agriculture was, thus, not a simple gift from god or a 'chance occurrence'; it came up as a result of human beings attempting to sort out their problems rather than succumbing to them. There is a rationale to all human developments that can be largely explained. History might have been an adjunct to theology at one point in time and even now is being used and abused by those in power, but today a student of history is trained to ascertain causes of historical processes without getting influenced from such quarters.

My efforts at reiterating centrality of causation and emphasis at empirical substantiation of historical arguments often bring in the issue of the role of chance. It was not surprising to find many students giving due importance to 'chance' in the questionnaire they filled in. Their argument was clear; so many events take place on which we have little control. The death of a leader in the political party can retard its fortunes. We attempt to reflect on it. What is chance? It is also known by other epithets such as 'the inevitable', an 'accident' or the 'inscrutable'. In his book *War and Peace*, Leo Tolstoy states that human beings are forced to fall back on fatalism as an explanation of irrational events when they can't understand the rationality of those events. Chance is not the 'inexplicable'; rather what has not been explained by those obliged to investigate. About things beyond our control, yes there appear to be some incidents that are strange and cannot be completely wished away. Alexander the Great's death at the young age of thirty-three as a result of a monkey bite or Lenin's death at a young age did impact the course of events in the future. However, a significant explanation of the course of events would not merit their inclusion beyond a casual reference. The break up of Alexander's empire can be explained in terms of not just his sudden death but the inability of the leader to consolidate the gains that he made instead of going on with more conquests. E.H.Carr associates emphasis on chance with a kind of 'intellectual laziness' or 'low intellectual vitality'. Accidents may not be immediately explicable but they can

even suburbs such as Ballabhgarh and they rub shoulders with friends from Delhi, Kolkata, Patna and Lucknow. However, there is an element of apprehension and insecurity on their arrival in the metropolis, more so if they have to settle in the city as paying guests. Their struggles are multitude, their stress levels high and this gets reflected in their level of participation in class discussions.

Quite a few first year students were reticent in responding to the exercise I undertook with them and were unwilling to fill in the questionnaire as well. To say the least they were laconic, not opening up to discussions. Most of the time the regular participants in such debates were Delhi-based students who had quickly formed their groups and were confident of negotiating their points. Students who came from the reserved backgrounds were reticent to acknowledge their social status on the paper, especially if they had the scope not to answer the query. On the question of how would the students want to be socially recognised they were prompt to adhere to their national identity. The relative unease with the exercise of social categorisation was palpable. The picture did change in the subsequent year. They were prepared to argue their case. By that time they had studied history of caste marginalisation and as one of them quipped later 'found their voice'. Besides, there were students who came from a Hindi medium background and stated in private conversations that they found it difficult to follow the lectures and were therefore hesitant in participating in either class discussions or what was written in the questionnaire. That is when I realised my own prejudice and started special tutorials with them. But what all of them concurred in was that their impression of the discipline was drastically different from what they encountered in their first year of the History Honours course.

On the issue of commonality between history and science their response was largely in the negative and they were genuinely confused about the possibility of comparing the disciplines. But they all readily agreed to revisit their views and impressions. That readiness to rethink on issues was encouraging and I also resolved to evolve my communicative and academic skills to keep pace with their expectations. My focus was clear; to evolve ways that would help them to negotiate their pressures and challenges better as students of history. I explained those ways in which a query needs to be comprehended and responded to. But most important it was essential to engage with them on historical interpretation, evidence and debate. Primary sources had to be introduced and relevance of reasoning emphasised in analysing the sources. There was the need to understand what historical writing or historiography was about along with developing the skill of evaluating/ critiquing a piece of historical writing. I asked them for suggestions that could help me spruce up my pedagogic skills. Some suggested that reading out material from primary textual sources and showing them how it could be used to develop a substantive historical argument would be of immense help. Some recommended the use of visual aids. One of the students form a Delhi school mentioned that her teacher had shown them the film *Schindler's List* as a part of their course on the Second World War and that had left an indelible imprint on her mind. It was a point well taken. Some suggested use of computers and visiting of relevant web sites. It was a good idea though I requested them to use caution as a lot of historical writing on the web is politically driven. We all agreed that regular paper presentations and organisation of seminars were other modes that could help us in becoming better students of history. The entire exercise was immensely enriching for me even as it was replete with challenges.

Let me add a few detailed responses of my second year students:

[A] 'I feel a change in the methodology of history teaching in college from the way it was being taught at school level.

History is no more a compendium of facts and dates rather it takes into cognisance the issue of time, space and fluctuations in social processes. Actual scientific techniques such as Carbon14 and paleontology are being used to assess dates of numerous events. We are taught distinct methodologies in analysing historical processes. Marxism is one such analytical tool that helps in understanding certain developments from the socio-economic perspective. Earlier history was a political narrative and that added to our boredom in attempting to learn it by rote. But the kinds of histories that we study today include tribal, regional and gender histories and these have assisted our understanding of the processes involved in numerous social formations; the emergence, mutations and collapse of simple and complex societies'.

'To a great extent I feel indebted to Marxist methodology in honing my analytical skills but at times I feel the overemphasis on economic rationale of so many issues takes away the relevance of other aspects such as the psychological aspect of human response to a given situation or the influence of ideas on the course of action. I have been wondering why so many Indian Jawans [soldiers] are committing suicides or murdering their seniors despite the fact that their salaries are good and their families being looked after. I also feel that the charisma of a leader can be at times greater than the background that throws him up. My plea is to make the discipline holistic and allow a variety of views to emerge on different issues. I also realise that it would be a long way before I can take sides in historical analysis but I hope I would have learnt my lesson well; to view others' point of view sympathetically'.

[B] 'At the school level, history seemed to be nothing but a collection of facts. There was hardly any scope of any kind of debate on any historical issue. It appeared extremely objective. It is only at the graduation level that history revealed its dynamic dimensions. I have learnt a simple fact; history is not only made by the actors of the period studied but by historians themselves. At the school level whatever appeared in our textbooks was the gospel truth. Today I realise that those writing that history are also human beings and products of a certain kind of thinking, so what surfaces in a book, is a reflection of one kind of history and histories can be written by many people from numerous vantages. Second, I have learnt the difference between a fact and a historical fact. A historical fact has to go through varied stages of scrutiny before it can be classified as a historical fact. Here we make use of scientific archaeological techniques and statistical textual analysis. But archaeology or a textual material alone does not recreate a historical fact. The pots cannot speak by themselves. Similarly, a lot of textual matter is mythical and in both cases the expertise of a trained historian is required equally for the selection of material of historical significance as well as its analysis. The same can be said of inscriptional and numismatic materials. Nothing goes as historical information without being checked over and over again.

'Historians have the additional responsibility of bringing forth 'unheard voices'. These could be of marginal sections of society who contributed in the making of history without having a hand in recording of it. Women, third gender, peasants, industrial labour all fall within this category. I believe that historians have the task of not just recreating the contexts of the existence of humanity but also study the mentalities of people. But the study has to be scientific as the issue can be quite subjective and may lead to overemphasis of just ideas without reflecting on the base. Somewhere the balance between the two needs to be secured. I consider history a scientific study of the past where the historian has to substantiate any case put forward both with evidence and a convincing argument. Any historical hypothesis has to stand the test of certain historical principles.'

[C] 'It has been almost two years of my encounter with

History Honours at the undergraduate level and my own comprehension of the discipline has undergone a sea change; from being, 'a mere study of dates and facts about the dead and the buried' to a more complete, comprehensive and enabling understanding of the past based on a rational, scientific and analytical examination of material available as well as varied interpretations. Today I have the courage to stand in the midst of a crowd and tell them that history is everything but a boring subject that induces sleep. It has allowed me to question, rationalise and frequently disagree with my teachers. The change that I am talking of is not a very personal experience. I vouch for the change in my friends' attitudes as well. We often discuss how the 'static' subject has become so dynamic. I share this discovery with the members of my family. I ask them not to speak of only one kind of history as there are many histories. I still remember that in the first year our teacher told us that there are as many histories as the number of historians. But we were also told that there is a methodology of differing. It required a certain degree of training before one can get equipped to put forth their views and to take in criticism.'

'History has also benefited from the changes that have appeared in other disciplines as our own discipline is becoming more interdisciplinary. We are openly borrowing new techniques of rationalising from Anthropology, Sociology, Mathematics and even Psychology. What I like about my discipline is its ability to grow. From a time when history was nothing but an objective study of dynasties, I think we have come a long way. We have changed our perspectives, made use of newer models and begun looking at the same material afresh. Revisiting the data and locating new dimensions which may often lead to changes in perspectives is not considered demeaning within the circle of historians. It is taken to be a sign of intellectual maturity. I proudly call history a scientific discipline because it permits itself to be questioned and does not take a stubborn recourse to stating that it reveals nothing but the absolute truth'.

The following is a sample copy of the questionnaire given to the students over two consecutive years, 2008-9 and 2009-10.

Perceptions on History and Expectations of First Year History Honours Students, Delhi University

Fill in the following details before answering the queries.

Name.

Last school attended.

Marks scored in the board examination.

Stream offered in Class XII examination.

Have you ever studied history as a distinct discipline? Specify the level up to which it was pursued.

Gender.

Specify whether you belong to SC/ST/OBC or any other category.

Queries

Mark the following in the order of preference. You may leave out the option you do not identify with. Alternatively you may add new options.

Issues of General Enquiry

1. What motivated you to opt for History Honours?
   a. Love for the discipline.
   b. Viewing it as an option for the UPSC and other competitive exams.
   c. Family persuasion.
   d. The only course available to you in the college of your preference.
2. What has been your source of studying history?
   a. School textbooks.
   b. School textbooks and those recommended by the teachers.
   c. Primary texts [could be translations].
   d. Field trips, visit to museums, archival material.

e. Newspaper and magazines.
f. Observation and discussions.

3. What fascinated you in the course of history at school level?
   a. Individuals such as Ashoka,the great, Akbar, Mahatma Gandhi, etc.
   b. Dynasties such as the Mughals in India, Tudors and Stuarts in England, etc.
   c. People's history for instance that of Santhals, Gujjars, Khasis and others.
   d. Genesis and development of the caste system in India.
   e. Important events such .
   f. Evolution of humanity and its progress through the prehistoric phase.
   g. History of colonialism and the National Movement.
   h. Cultural history/histories.
4. What are your expectations of the course [BA Honours or Programme] over the next three years? Would you continue to study the above or widen your horizons in the following areas?
   a. Gender studies.
   b. History of genesis of classes, class consciousness and movements.
   c. Role of environment and technology in historical development.
   d. Family histories.
   e. Regional histories.
   f. History of communities such as the Sikhs, Marathas, etc.
   g. History of religion.
5. What in your opinion is social science?
   a. It is another name for social studies taught at school level.
   b. It is the science of society.

   c. A discipline that equips an individual with analytical skills to study social categories and changes in society over time and space.
6. How would you want to be socially identified?
   a. By the family name.
   b. By your caste.
   c. The region you hail from.
   d. The religion you follow.
   e. National identity.

Issues of Historical Enquiry

7. What is history?
   a. A compendium of facts and dates.
   b. A discipline to encourage rational thinking.
   c. An enquiry into the past with an eye on the present.
   d. A social science that helps an individual to comprehend social issues over time and space.
8. What is a historical fact?
   a. Anything that has happened in the past.
   b. A fact to which the historians impute relevance that is something which is debated upon.
   c. Historical fact is what the power wielding individuals decide should be told to posterity. It is selective in nature and beneficial to some individuals/groups in society.
9. How should history be periodised?
   a. On the basis of chronology [large time spans].
   b. On the basis of dynasties.
   c. On the basis of social formations.
   d. On the basis of important events.
10. In your opinion how objective should historical explorations and assimilations be?
   a. Should be based on empirical evidence alone [Dates and facts based] and should primarily be a bald narrative of events,
   b. Should be a combination of a study of empirical

data to create events along with their rational analysis that underline the causative function of the discipline.

c. Should also make room for reflection on personal biases, social environment that influence both the collection of data and its interpretation,

11. How much importance would you give to 'chance' or 'accident' in analysing historical developments? Or how central is causation to understanding historical processes?
    a. Historical events cannot be explained in terms of general laws because 'the chapter accidents' and 'chance coincidence' enter into historical processes [J.S.Bury].
    b. 'Chance' in history is said to 'accelerate' or 'retard' but not radically alter the course of events [Karl Marx] [by implication not too much importance is laid on it for seeking historical implication].
    c. 'Accident' or 'chance' is merely a measure of our ignorance; simply a name for something that we fail to understand [Leo Tolstoy].
    d. The accidental sequence does not belong to the historian's hierarchy of significant causes; it does not enter into any rational interpretation of history [hence should be rejected for historical explanations, (E.H.Carr)].
12. Can history be associated with predictive accuracy?
    a. No it cannot be as historical paradigms are not testable.
    b. Yes it can be. So many wars have almost been predicted.
    c. There may not be predictive accuracy as in the case of pure sciences but it may be possible to predict similar situations by studying comparable historical circumstances.
13. What is the role of an individual in society?

a. An individual [also referred to as a great man] can be a prime mover and steer social and historical events in a certain direction.
b. An individual is merely a product of a certain social set up and hence a conscious or unconscious spokesman of the society he or she belongs to.
c. A great man or woman in history is always representative either of existing forces or of forces which he helps to create/ mould by the way of challenge to existing authority.
d. A great man/ woman is an individual who is at once a product and agent of the historical process, at once the representative of and the creator of social forces which change the shape of the world and thoughts of humanity.

14. In your opinion what is religion?
    a. A highly personalised belief system that vests faith in what is perceived as a force/ power above human capabilities and which needs to be propitiated.
    b. A system evolved by some to ensure their social supremacy.
    c. A belief system that lends its community of followers its identity and cohesion.

Write your views on the following issues:

15. Can history be abused by those in power for political ends?
16. What is the difference between Social Science and History?
17. Is historical truth verifiable?
18. How objective can one be in historical assessment?

4

Communicating History: A Classroom Experience

Pradeep Kant Choudhary

The pedagogical questions related to communicating history at the school level have generated a limited but heated debate in India for so many years, especially in the context of the NCERT syllabi being revised time and again.[1] However, there is complete absence of any serious discussion on the pedagogical aspects of teaching history at the college and university levels. Academic establishments including we the teachers are far less sensitive to the issues of developing a learner-centric education system and we rarely discuss the issues of the learning goal and overall course load of the students. It seems that our curricula are developed according to the interest of teachers involved in the curricula drafting committees without understanding the nature and characteristics of the learner. In fact, now the University of Delhi has even started the practice of imposing a curriculum prepared by somewhat unconcerned 'experts' sitting inside closed doors meetings with no questions asked, no debates conducted.

Curricula framers are often expected to confront several questions and dilemmas. Is the space available for proposed curricula finite or infinite? What should be the level of imparting both breadth and depth of courses' formulations?

We also face the questions regarding the broad goals of teaching history such as the ways to inculcate the ability to explain the present, or to locate the common people in the long march of human development; or to understand the significance of the specificities of temporal and spatial contexts affecting such developments in different time frames and places. Skills to comprehend logic and logistics of factors inhibiting the course/s of historical processes involving change and continuities come within the realm of the learner-centric history curricula at the undergraduate level.

History teachers have many challenges before them. Encountering a bunch of students still in their teens and burdened with received notions of 'non-utilitarian' character of this discipline presents perhaps one of the most important of such challenges. Making students aware of the relevance of studying history, its policy implications, history's place in the community of social sciences, and its utility in understanding the conflicts of society are quite helpful intellectual goals of learners. If they could be made to perceive themselves as guardians of collective memory, custodians of cultural heritage and important contributors of policy making, that might make them better learners.

Locating and understanding the extremely varied social, economic, cultural and economic milieu of learners inside the classroom is a strong imperative of communicating history. Teachers should understand the specificities of learners – their gender, social affiliations, spatial linkages (whether one belongs to a metropolitan town or a rural hinterland or economically backward regions), and so on. For example, our experience shows that our best students are those who did not study history in school. Perhaps it is equally true that those who had studied history at the +2 level are better served when they unlearn such histories as are taught at the Senior Secondary level of schools. The approach and perspectives of history communication at school is qualitatively different from the undergraduate programme at the university. The school teaching generally has a mere fact-oriented approach with objective type short answers dominating their studies. Rarely do they follow an analytical method to understand history as a tool of understanding social changes in the past. Many of the inquisitive minds get bored, biased and feel humiliated at an early age and suffer from an inferiority complex – the extant social values tend to ostracise them, 'humanities types' being juxtaposed to superior 'science types'.

Sometimes a relaxed attitude –like history is an 'easy discipline' and we will do it when exams come or 'lack of challenge' for a new discipline becomes big obstacles for these students. Apparently the popularly perceived notion that this discipline provides a useful gateway for entering the glamorous world of the Indian Civil Services (IAS, IPS, IFS, etc.) is perhaps the only allurement that tends to sustain their feeble interest. As far as the teachers are concerned, some take it as a challenge but in most other cases, the general lackadaisical attitude of students and their distaste for the discipline become counter-productive. The one factor that keeps teachers going is the strong motivation of the less privileged, socially degraded and economically deprived students. Surprisingly, more often than not, such motivated learners come from the so-called 'bad', 'government' schools and often outshine the more privileged ones reared through the capital investments in the so-called 'good' and 'private' schools.

It seems that two inter-related exercises make the task of developing a learner-centric instructions viable enterprise in this regard. First, the need to communicate immense relevance of the subject. Second, conducting a dialogue between the past and the present in the classroom conditions by taking up such issues of caste, class, gender, regions, identities, etc., which may lead to widening of perspectives of the world around these young minds. These twin pathways of communicating history involve an establishment of a true partnership between the teacher and the taught. A strong case for a dialogue between the two is a must if history as a dialogue between the past and present is to be crystallised. Since the word of the teacher is sometimes taken as almost the 'gospel truth' (by many students, if not all) it imposes a colossal responsibility on the shoulders of the teachers. We have known a teacher who once said in the presence of many professional colleagues: *"hum to Maurya samrajya ke patan ke karan padhate padhate hi retire ho jayenge."* (we shall be retiring after teaching the causes of the decline of the Mauryan Empire year after year.) We dare not defend such colleagues – irrespective of their growing numbers. Nor are we pretending that all teachers function with a messianic zeal and act as life changers. But certainly, some sparks here and there, some involvement with the students and display of even microscopic concern for the learners can infuse some quality in their lives. Encouraging students to ask questions can go a long way in inculcating some basic strands of historical discipline. History is a discipline of reason — this basic lesson needs to be internalised by history learners at the earliest possible stage of their learning career. My own area of interest, spanning over two decades — both in teaching and research — being in early/ancient Indian history (conveniently demarcated with terminal chronological points around the end of the 12th century CE), places me in a somewhat advantageous position. It provides useful entry points to instructors like me whereby the proverbial dialogue between the past and the present becomes feasible and the utility of history as a discipline gets legitimacy and credibility.

One area that has phenomenal potential to generate interest and ignite the inquisitive and curious minds is concerned with the issue of gender construction. This also happens to be an area that has come under arc lights in the last three decades or so and provides fruitful insights to undertake a dialogue between the past and the present. A phenomenon that often baffles learners of both sexes in general and women in particular is concerned about the dichotomy between an extremely exalted status in the world of divinities and an equally despicable status of women on the ground, i.e. in actual daily life. Delving into the roots of this phenomenon with the help of insights drawn from material evidences unearthed by archaeologists as well as through re-reading of literary and epigraphic texts is an exercise that turns out to be very rewarding. Learners find it quite exciting that initially, the physical differences between men and women were not many and that both were equally robust, at least till such times when humans were not engaged in producing their food and survived on hunting and food gathering. The advent of agriculture marks the beginning of the process when women tended to lose their height and muscular power. With women confining themselves to child rearing and domestic field cultivation and men setting out for the hardy life of hunting perhaps marks the beginning of the notion of women being a 'weaker sex'. Studies in the Primate Societies suggest that unequal access to food played a crucial role in this. The men tended to consume the bulk of hunted animals or ate the collected roots and fruits at the site itself and women had to rest contented with the mere leftovers. Perhaps the image of women as mere nurturers rather than producers of wealth as well, goes back to such prehistoric times.

Similarly there are occasions to discuss how women were relegated to private spaces of their household, while much of public space was being occupied by men, specially after the emergence of class society. Notwithstanding the recent realisation that at the level of royalty, some queens, princesses, etc. show their involvement in matters of state and that women donors of money, gifts, etc. to brahmanical and non-brahmanical establishments came to the fore since the dawn of the Common Era, the overall picture eloquently tells us that this unequal access to public space is the root cause of gender inequality. It helps us to explain that even in the field of cooking when there is an opportunity in the public spheres like village feasts, men occupy the centre-stage. Otherwise in modern day festivities, marriages and in hotels and highway eateries there would not have been any male chef (in the five star hotels, they are armed with hotel management degrees and work on hefty salaries) and their wives silently cooking at home. In ancient India we find that learning music and art for women were also confined to private spaces and performing in public was looked down upon – *ganikas, devadasis*, etc. were socially degraded people. Even in the field of religion women could not be treated with equality. An enlightened religion like Buddhism prescribed that nuns could not be teachers of monks. It clearly shows that even great men are trapped in their own times as we find in the case of the Buddha's view on the question of women joining the Buddhist *Sangha* (the monastic order). Saddling women with ignoble practices such as *sati* and *niyoga* and imposing upon them a rigorous regime of *vratas* (almost throughout the year) were subtle devices that sought to perpetuate patriarchal social order. When learners of history are informed that gender construction is not natural but social, it generates newer curiosities and students are able to see the potentials of studying history as the meaningful tool of social transformation.

Changes in the social structure through the millennia are yet another area whereby learner-centric history communication can relate the past with the present. This is certainly a domain where students' notions about class and caste can be located and many of their burdens unloaded. In the current Indian milieu of caste-centred politics, students are somewhat shy of expressing their caste identities. Knowledge of the formation of such identities in a specific historical context tends to encourage the young learner to open up. Thus, demythification of the 'divine' origin of the caste system, of the notions of purity of blood, of inherent superiority of brahmanas and criteria of pollution make considerable sense to him/her. That there was indeed considerable class-caste mobility and that there were numerous examples of transgressions of expected social behaviour often get a very positive reception in the socially diverse classroom.

Encouraging students to ask simple questions about long persisting stereotypes further help them in comprehending the dynamics of social order. Did all the kings and the ruling elite belong to the kshatriya varna as laid down by the brahmanical order? The fact that many ruling dynasties in ancient India such as the Nandas, Mauryas, Shungas, Guptas, Kushanas, Satavahanas, Cholas, Hoysalas, etc. were of non-kshatriya or perhaps even shudra (modern day Dalits) origins is enough to break such stereotypes. It also helps students to comprehend such dynamic processes as are involved in '*Rajputisation*' of some tribal chiefs of uncertain origins. The most important phenomenon of medieval centuries (6th–13th centuries), viz. fabrication of glorious genealogies tracing origins of many kings to epic heroes of 'solar' and 'lunar' families also gets demystified in course of such searching questions.

Similarly, various issues related to the origin of brahmana clans and groups help them to appreciate the historical evolution of the Indian social order. Just like other communities, brahmanas were also made of heterogeneous groups originating from different backgrounds. There are oral traditions in western India about how Parashurama converted fishermen into brahmanas and how he made sacred threads out of fishing nets. Right from the Vedic period we find appropriation of a large number of the local priestly order into various clans of brahmanas. We have examples of people like Dirghataṃas and many other Vedic seers who had 'non-Aryan' or 'non-Sanskritic' social roots.

Vishwamitra and Vasishtha legends are classic examples of inter-changeability of brahmana-kshatriya status. The brahmanical law books tell us that if brahmanas married shudra women then their son should get some share, albeit lower, in the property of his brahmana father. The question is that if such marriages were accommodated inside the strict social norms, then how could their claim about the purity of blood remain valid?

The battle of and battle for the most downtrodden sections of the society poses perhaps one of the most difficult challenges for the communicator of historical pasts. Writings on Indian history have been a considerable semantic burden. Thus use of 'Shudra' has become not only unparliamentary but almost a taboo as well. Even the Gandhian formulation for them, viz. 'harijan' is not a preferred one and has gone out of vogue. Currently, 'dalit' has become the most politically correct expression, notwithstanding the fact that varied textual traditions across India and across several millennia are unfamiliar with it. This then presents a dilemma for the professional historians, who would hate the idea of fabricating the facts. Semantic fineness apart, young impressionistic learners also need to be taken through the complex web of intersecting axes of both caste and class. The last few decades of the so-called 'backward caste' politics in contemporary India has given rise to the unquantifiable notion of the 'creamy layer' within such groupings. The question needs to be asked: does upward mobility (both political and economic) of some individuals of a given caste or tribe *ipso facto* implies similar mobility of the whole class to which those individuals belong? Further, does economic and political mobility also ensure social rise of the concerned in the same direction? It is frequently seen that answers to such questions are often in the negative. An apt historical illustration would be that Mahapadma Nanda, the founder of the Nanda dynasty, which preceded that of the more famous dynasty of the Mauryas. Mahapadma Nanda is supposed to have been of a very low social origin (perhaps in a shudra class) who rose to become a king by sheer dint of his military prowess. The dharmashastric texts following this development refuse to provide any respectable space for that class which continued to be saddled with numerous social, economic and educational disabilities. With such historical insights would it not be relevant to ask whether the salvation of 'dalits' lies in the individual success or in the real changes in the social order consequent upon new production relations?

Historically speaking, the formation of regions and regional identities is a very complex phenomenon. In today's parlance, the notions of 'backward regions', 'sick areas' , 'the mainstream', 'the outlying regions', 'tribal pockets', etc. have become sources of social tensions. Many such pulls and pressures end up with a sense of alienation, which in turn, tends to foment violent fissiparous tendencies. The policy planners of modern times, who grapple with problems of cultural integration, economic imbalances, and sharing of economic resources, etc., can take a leaf or two out of the processes involved in the emergence of regional identities. The roots of more than ninety eco-cultural zones (some of the big states have multiple zones) that have been identified by the 'People of India' project of the Anthropological Survey of India can be traced back to the very remote past. By early medieval times (say around the beginning of the second millennium CE) evidence of different cultural zones with their specific material bases, linguistic and literary peculiarities, dresses and hair styles, artistic tastes, etc. becomes obvious. Such insights demolish the myth of any homogeneous cultural identity. Instead, contributions of various groups and communities in creating a pluralistic cultural rainbow stare at us. Even in pre and proto-historic times Gandhara grave culture shows plurality of cultural traditions. In fact, various centres of Harappan civilization have different religious orientations incorporating the possibilities of the fire cult, the mother goddess cult, the proto-Shiva cult and diverse animistic practices. Unity in diversity is not a mere slogan constructed by our freedom fighters, but this is how India has existed from prehistoric times. Communication of such material data should help in mitigating feelings of alienation which is so pronounced amongst numerous tribal communities of India. Further, the role of brahmanas, who detested manual labour and any entrepreneurial activities, can be properly assessed to get to the social roots of economic backwardness – not with a spirit of rancour towards them but with a positive orientation of comprehending the complexities of social dynamics.

Finally, how does one communicate the significance of the material evidence of 'cultural capital' strewn all over east, west and south-east Asia? These are available in monumental remains, linguistic and literary vestiges, religious identities in these regions (for example, the presence of Buddhism and other Indian religions) and so on. The earlier generations of historians took considerable pride in identifying such 'Indian colonies,' wrote about India's 'cultural empire/imperialism' and even identified so-called 'Greater India'. Evidently, such historical constructions are outdated. The students, when sensitised about the need to understand this 'Cultural Capital' left by our forefathers, are able to juxtapose this phenomenon to the modern day effort of power like China. They are also able to understand ASEAN and the spirit of *Panchsheel* better. Instead of remaining moored in the mode of 'Glorious India' efforts need to be directed towards rationalisation of the phenomenon.

NOTES

1. For critical analyses of issues involved in these debates, see, Krishna Mohan Shrimali, 'Scientific Communication and History Writing'—Paper presented at the First Peoples

Education Congress held at Allahabad in September 2005 and published in N.P.Chaubey and Sushma, eds. *Science Communication*, Peoples Council of Education, 2009, pp. 142-85; *Idem*, "Whither Social History?" General President's Address, *Proceedings of the 38th Session (2006) of the Punjab History Congress*, Punjabi University, Patiala, 2007, pp. 6-35. A slightly revised version of the latter has been included in this volume.

5

Scientific History: The Writing and Teaching of Social Studies in Schools

Shalini Shah

This paper will analyse the concept of scientific history, as also the teaching of this history, as part of the social studies curriculum in schools.

I

The discipline of history began as 'inquiry', for this is the meaning of the Greek term *histor*, which Herodotus (who is recognised as the father of history) used in his work. For Herodotus, history was not legend or myth,[1] but rather it was research into human action, and the objective of this history was human self-knowledge. It was, thus, not theocratic but humanistic.

However, this legacy of a human-centred, research-based corpus of knowledge was lost sight of, and during the Middle Ages history was reduced to being a hand-maiden of theology. The idea that history conforms to a purposive principle, and that this principle has its sources in the wisdom of God, is implied in the conception of the past set forth by St. Augustine. This Augustinian tradition continued to flourish for more than a thousand years. It was in the 17th-18th century that a salvage operation began to rescue history from the clutches of theologians and, thereby, to jettison religious and metaphysical metaphors concerning human affairs. It was Voltaire who in the 18th century coined the term philosophy of history, by which he meant an independent and critical thinking. Throughout the 19th century the efforts of scholars was to create a historically valid social and historical science. This was the objective of people like Condorcet, J.S. Mill, Marx and Engels, all of whom though in widely varying ways were wedded to the belief that the application of scientific procedures to the study of human affairs was a realisable possibility.

Yet even in the 19th century when beliefs of this sort were at their height there were critics like Arthur Schopenhauer and Jacob Burckhardt who challenged the optimistic and rationalistic pre-supposition upon which the view of a universal historical science was based, and cast doubt upon the idea that the subject matter of history (the human being) was amenable to such treatment. Man, after all, is the biggest variable. Furthermore, the complexity and particularity of individual historical occurrences does not permit its sub-sumption under universal laws. For German scholar J.G. von Herder, the human action was not a product of unchanging human consciousness; rather it was mediated by the temporal, spatial and cultural contexts.

In the 19th century there were scholars who were of the view that till history was seen as a mode of disseminating moral lessons, it would never be seriously taken as a scientific discipline. Thus, Ranke in his protest against morals in history remarked that the task of history was "simply to show how it really was". The positivists who were anxious to stake out their claim for history as a science, contributed the weight of their influence to this 'cult of facts'. However, what these scholars failed to appreciate was that for a fact to become or be treated as historical fact, some measure of interpretation is necessary, and the historian who interprets is bound to make some value judgments. There is, thus, no 'pure' historical fact outside the historian's mind.[2] The historian, says R.G. Collingwood, not only re-enacts past thought, he re-enacts it in the context of his own knowledge and, therefore, in re-enacting it criticises it, forms his own judgment of its value ... this criticism of the thought whose history he traces is not something secondary to tracing the history of it, rather it is an indispensable condition of the historical knowledge itself. Collingwood, therefore, wanted the discipline of history to be released from the state of its pupilage to 'natural science', where the emphasis is on the discovery of some universal law that could explain a natural phenomenon. Nonetheless, while the mode of explanation of physical science and history may vary, E.H. Carr states that historians and physical scientists are all united in the fundamental purpose of seeking to explain, and in the fundamental procedure of question and answer. The object of the two is also the same – to increase man's understanding of, and mastery over, the environment.

II

Soon after India's independence in 1947, as Indian education was preparing to meet the challenge of nurturing young minds, one of the significant pedagogical issues for the educationists was how to impart a consciousness of the past to these children. Inculcating the scientific temper was something that Nehru had always stressed. So, in the context of the writing of history books this was taken to mean a rationalist, material approach, where the religious perspective of any denomination was to be completely eschewed. This was particularly relevant in a country which not only had thousands of years old civilization, but was also a melting pot of numerous ethnic, linguistic and religious communities. A historical narrative which would be subjective[3] in any way, could not be included in recommended textbooks which were, after all, meant for children from all walks of life. What, then, was to be a common basis for inquiry into the historical past? Since in the post-independence era Marxist writings in history were becoming significant, and given the socialist leanings of political leadership, a history of culture and civilisation that concentrated on the economic dynamics, looked at the marginals and dealt with the political narratives in terms of class groupings tended to paper-over the sensitive issues of ethnic/religious differences. This comes through very strongly in Satish Chandra's treatment of the Rajput and Maratha interface with the Mughals in the 1980s NCERT textbooks on medieval India.

So for a few decades after independence the school textbooks on history were written to give expression to avowed national aims of unity in diversity, secularism and social equity. During the late 1990s this pedagogical consensus gave way to a new agenda of 'identity formation'; an identity which was to be a 'pure' one, shorn of its acculturation over many hundreds of years. This period in the writing of textbooks has been referred to as the 'saffronisation' of education.

In the last five years NCERT has come out with a new set of textbooks on history where the group of eminent historians who have been associated with its writing have tried to bring centre-stage (what was only implicit in the earlier decades) and to unravel the various nuances of the historian's craft for the impressionable young minds. This was particularly important, as in the era of 'saffronisation' what was being conveyed to the young readers, their guardians and the general public (through propaganda in the press and media) was that history was nothing more than an ideological trip. The new textbook had to demonstrate, so to speak, how an objective methodology was followed in dealing with the sources. Thus, the new textbooks took great care in quoting from the primary sources directly, be it the Ashokan edicts, the *Mahabharata*, Amir Khusrau's couplets, or the Mughal *farmans* and the medieval miniature paintings. Space for this was made in especially constructed 'boxes of information' and the reader was encouraged to draw his/her conclusions from it. Another methodological approach which the new textbooks adopted was to bring the idea of perspective in the interpretation of historical events. In the class IX textbook, which dealt with some major periods of European history, in the discussion on the French Revolution, students were made virtual participants in examining the question 'Did women have a revolution?'. This issue was sought to be examined from the angle of women's participation in the events of the French Revolution, as also the ideological leadership provided by them. Thus, while the traditional historiographical narrative of the French Revolution was kept intact, simultaneously the gender perspective in the reading of this internationally significant historical event was fruitfully introduced for the young minds to grasp.

Another important pedagogical issue for the writers was the kind of subject matter in history that should be taken up. In other words, is the study of authoritative institutions or regimes in power the end-all and be-all of history? Hegel once noted that in history only those people can come under our notice who form a state. The new textbooks, however, chose to sensitise children to a new kind of history; a history which was not merely a discourse of power, but one where ordinary people's material existence and their cultural transactions were valid subjects for historical analysis. Concerns about ecology and the environment were woven into the class IX history books in the discussion on peasants, pastoralists and forest-dwellers. Children were introduced to the manner in which cultural history is recorded by discussion on the history of cricket as it emerged in England. How this 'gentleman's game' was embedded in the class consciousness of a stratified society where the amateurs/gentlemen were mostly all batsmen[4] while the professional players drawn from the more plebian strata of society (many of whom were mine workers) not only did the job of bowling but also entered the playing field from a different gate which was reserved for them. Needless to say, the position of cricket captain was the preserve of the titled gentlemen. Even the rules of the game reflected this class bias, where the benefit of the doubt was always given in favour of the batsmen and not the bowler.

Attire is something that is a commonplace in life, yet there is little else which has been as fraught with symbolism or has been the locus of much social and civil legislation as clothes. In Europe of the *ancien regime* only the royalty and aristocracy were entitled to bedeck themselves in ermine and fur. In India men wore a head-dress which proclaimed their caste identity. The untouchables went bare-foot and bare-bodied. It is, therefore, significant that in colonial India while Gandhi took to wearing a *langot* to proclaim his solidarity with the common masses, the Dalit Ambedkar wore a three-piece Western suit to equally make the point about how an equal opportunity for education and employment could act as a revolutionary catalyst in changing the life of the oppressed and marginals in Indian society.

III

This section of the paper deals not so much with the pedagogical issues per se, but rather seeks to share with the readers my experience as a mother helping a young son with his preparation of Social Studies.

Till class VIII the Social Studies textbook in school is a more general book which includes lessons from three major streams, viz., History, Civics and Geography. One common refrain from my son as also some of his friends with whom I interacted was 'SST is a bore', this of course reminded me of my own school days when a common Hindi proverb which was repeated with some vehemence of emotions was *History, Geography badi bewafa, raat ko padho subah ko safa.*

Writing about this I feel that at least in early classes, in terms of both writing of the textbooks and teaching it some space and time can be devoted to re-creating [say a historical period] rather than heavy interpretive passages. For example, if the chapter is on the Mauryas a map of the Indian subcontinent with sites of Ashokan edicts be shown and 2-3 lines of the famous Kalinga edict can be translated word for word with letters from the Brahmi script shown with their modern equivalent in Hindi. It will also be exciting for students if visually the route of Alexander of Macedon's eastward march into the Indian subcontinent is traced with Greek soldiers in their tunics and head gear. What I have in mind here is 25-30 minutes visual lessons on the CDs which are played out to the students before formal lessons from the book on that topic is covered. I personally found Shyam Benegal's *Bharat ek Khoj* television series as also specific *Amar Chitra Katha* (illustrated story books) series very useful in generating interest in my son.

Similarly, historical characters/personalities can be brought closer to young children's consciousness in various ways. For example, Akbar need not be presented only as a formidable Mughal emperor, rather interesting historical information but in a lighter vein [if not in the meta narrative at least in the box at the corner of the chapter] can be recorded which would stay with children for a long while. Just the other day I was reading an interesting book by Professor Shireen Moosvi titled *Episodes in the Life of Akbar* where she cites a contemporary record by a Persian visitor to Agra fort who was amazed to see the twenty-year-old Mughal emperor Akbar flying a kite on the roof of his palace wearing merely a *lungi* with head uncovered.

In geography, too, the lessons on climate and vegetations of the regions and the subsistence patterns of various ecological zones can be made more interesting by showing children tundra vegetation, deciduous forests, people engaged in earning a livelihood in the desert region and so on visually.

While doing civics lesson on the Directive Principles of the State Policy, my son came across terms like abolition of untouchability, progressive discrimination, etc. For a cosmopolitan city bred boy, with socially conscious educated parents, the notion of untouchability was a concept totally alien to him. It is here that a screening of Satyajit Ray's tele-film *Sadgati* would have helped as also reading aloud in the class, passages from Premchand's story *Thakur ka Kuan*.

Apart from untouchability, some other terms which foxed him were gender inequality and gender discrimination. Even when the text explained the former concepts as unequal rights for men and women, and the latter as discrimination against females in the spheres of education, employment, etc. he found it difficult to comprehend them. As far as he could see there were girls in school, and if his father went to work so did his mother. So what was the fuss about?

Gender inequality/discrimination is not the kind of concept that can be explained to young school boys as slogans. They need to be sensitised by patiently tracing the history of gender discrimination by bringing to their notice myriad examples from daily life. Undesirability of girls can be forcefully established by giving to them lopsided sex ratio figures in India. Statistics are something which children of all age groups understand easily and then on the basis of figures, the discrimination aspect can be underlined.

As an academic teaching one of the SST subjects, i.e. history, I have a personal stake in seeing to it that bright young children do not find SST a big bore!

NOTES

1. A historian begins by asking a question, whereas a narrator of myths/legends such as Homer begins by telling what he knows.
2. Nonetheless it needs to be remembered, as Carr reminds us, that while no historian can claim for his own values an

objectivity beyond history, an objective historian can be said to be one with a capcity to rise above the limited vision of his own situation in society and in history, and with the capacity to project his vision into the future in such a way as to give him a more profound and a more lasting insight into the past.

3. History is notorious for being the account of the victors and the dominant.
4. It is interesting to note that all the Indian cricketers who came from royal families like Ranjit Singh, Duleep Singh and Mansur Ali Khan Pataudi were also batsmen.

6

Teaching Social History (**)

K.M. Shrimali

In this presentation we intend sharing our deep concern about the directions of teaching and writing social history, specially at the pre-University level. In our enthusiasm to display our erudition, we have often neglected such analyses in our deliberations at various academic and professional fora.

There are two interrelated aspects of social history which have come to the fore in recent years that need attention. First, attempts to scrutinise and eliminate such writings that seek to be critical of the brahmanical view of history. Such attempts have pandered to the cries of the faithful and tended to muzzle voices of reason, which ought to provide the bedrock of historical discipline. Second, under the garb of studying 'popular culture' and perhaps also under the influence of the *avant-garde* 'post-modernism', the emergent trend is to underplay the dynamics of India's social fabric.

There are three sets of documents that need to be looked at. These are [a] *The National Curriculum Framework for School Education* published by the National Council of Educational Research and Training (NCERT) in 2000 (hereafter *NCF*) and corresponding history syllabi for classes VI to XII [b] the directive from the Central Board of Secondary Education (CBSE) issued in 2001, and [c] *The National Curriculum Framework 2005* also published by the NCERT (hereafter

NCF-05) and corresponding history syllabi for classes VI to XII. We shall undertake a review of these insofar as they are manifestations of a certain kind of social history. Ours is not an exercise of reviewing history textbooks for various pre-University classes in different parts of India. However, certain important extracts will have to be cited in order to underline the contours and possible directions of that kind of history.

I

The Bombay High Court in Anant Janardan Karandikar *vs* State observed in 1967: "It is the right and privilege of every thinker to express his judgment on historical events in a fearless manner. Otherwise, we will not get a true and faithful history of our country. History is not to serve as a handmaid of a particular school of thought...To rewrite history according to the views which are popular or which are necessary for bolstering up nationalistic egoism or jingoism, is perversion of history."

The two *NCF*s belie hopes raised by such an unalloyed plea for a reasoned enquiry in history writing, which is increasingly coming under the public domain. Historical scholarship today seemingly faces a peculiar choice: history by litigation or history by fiat. The *NCF*, calling itself 'Frontline Curriculum'[1] became notorious for seeking to perpetuate several divides, viz. class/caste; rural and urban; brahmanic/Sanskritic *vs* non-brahmanic/non-Sanskritic and, of course, the great divide of genders. Examples of such divides could be seen in the following formulations:

(i) About 'Education of Girls' : "It will be most appropriate to recognise and nurture the best features of each gender in the best Indian tradition"[2] — this is an insidious move towards pushing women's education back from even notions of equal educational opportunities.

(ii) On 'Vocational Education': "The vocational education programme [is] designed to meet the varying needs of the socially disadvantaged groups, such as women, scheduled castes, scheduled tribes and physically challenged persons, would help them acquire suitable productive skills...competency based curricula..."[3] – this is clearly a caste-oriented formulation with an implicit assumption that people belonging to the disadvantaged sections of society are inherently deficient in acquiring higher skills and, therefore, deserve only a particular type of education (one may recall some such arguments at the height of the anti-Mandalisation movement of the late 1980s).

(iii) On 'Environment and Community as Resources': "Environment, both rural and urban, and community are great resources for curriculum development. The vastness and openness of the serene rural environment with its fields, forests, ponds, rivers, trees, orchards, birds and animals is a major provider to curriculum development. Similarly, the busy business centres, industrial complexes, neat and clean residential clusters and not so clean and not so healthy slum areas of cities provide a different kind of input to the process of curriculum making. Flexibility of procedures, instructional materials and instructional arrangements supported by training and enrichment materials for teachers prepared by the local educational institutions and authorities can easily provide the requisite rich local input of the environmental resources in the curriculum...."[4]

(iv) On 'Education for Value Development': "Schools can and must strive to restore and sustain the *universal and eternal* values oriented towards the unity and integration of the people, their moral and spiritual growth enabling them to realise the treasure within... Self-recognition would come to them through proper value education that would facilitate their spiritual march from the level of sub-consciousness top to that of super consciousness through the different intermediary stages. Value-based education would help the nation fight against all kinds of fanaticism, ill will, violence, fatalism, dishonesty, avarice, corruption, exploitation and drug abuse."[5] (*emphases added*). It may be legitimately asked if the invocation of the so-called universal and eternal values meant only brahmanical values. After all, many of the non-brahmanical systems, specially Buddhism, discarded all forms of eternalism and stood for values of constant change. Did this concern for value education also mean continuation of the iniquitous social order? Let us not forget that whenever the new social forces challenged the brahmanical social order, the priestly order and the ruling elite combined to speak about the virtues and need of the varna order–*varna vyavasthaapanaa* – establishment of the varna order was regarded as the principal duty of the king. Finally, this call for sustaining universal and eternal values was geared towards only people's 'moral and spiritual growth'. Where is the concern for the material growth of people? Or is it assumed that such a growth could be achieved through an unscrupulous value system as we see too often in our contemporary daily lives.

(v) That the intent of the curriculum framers was to perpetuate brahamanical bias may also be seen in the provisions about teaching of Sanskrit. "Sanskrit has a special claim on the national system of education because it has consistently been needed in India [*sic*] for thousands of years and is still inextricably linked with the life, rituals, ceremonies and festivals of the vast Indian masses;... has the universal appeal all over the country... has been internationally accepted as the most scientifically structured language and is being increasingly acknowledged as the best suited language for computer use... the language is to be treated as a living phenomenon which is still relevant to the general life needs of the people of India, and which has caught international attention because of the global interest in subjects like yoga, Vedic mathematics, astronomy and Ayurveda."[6]

II

NCF and History Syllabi

History formed part of the social science curricula in the upper primary and secondary stages (classes VI-X), whereas, it was sought to be developed as an independent discipline in the senior secondary stages (classes XI-XII) under the *NCF*. The rationale and objectives of these formulations have been worked out in very laudable terms. Categorically laying down that the "teaching of social sciences must be objective, based on scientific enquiry, and free from all kinds of stereotyped images, biases and prejudices", the major objectives tended to focus on:

(i) Studying the past in its context; understanding and appreciating the diversities in lands and peoples of India and the world, and the interdependence of regions and countries; an appreciation of the richness and variety of India's heritage – both natural and cultural and the need for its preservation.

(ii) Developing an awareness of the various social and economic challenges before the country.

(iii) Acquiring necessary abilities and skills, both academic and social, which would enable the learner to differentiate between fact/fiction, and would help her/him to think critically and creatively, communicate effectively, cooperate with others and respond to the needs of others.

(iv) Developing scientific temper by promoting the spirit of enquiry and following a rational and objective approach in analysing and evaluating data and information as well as views and interpretations ['inculcation of scientific temper' integral to components of the National Policy on Education, 1986].

(v) Studying local historical developments in a broader countrywide and worldwide context. Such studies with their inter-connections with the broader world would act as an antidote to bigotry, parochialism, communalism and regional cultural chauvinism...

A perusal of syllabi of history shows that many of these formulations were mere empty words. Exposition of rudiments and rubrics of social history would perhaps be the best illustration of the hollowness of the aforesaid ideals. The words 'society' and 'social conditions' rarely went beyond stereotypical and ritualistic enumerations. One is left with utter disbelief to find that the emergence of *setthis* and the *gahapatis* as a new social force during the phase of the dispersal of iron technology in the Ganga valley and their links with the growth and proliferation of urban centres between *circa* 600 and *circa* 200 BCE were conspicuous by their absence. The 'Iron Age' was expected to be understood only in the context of the 'Deccan and South India'. We suspect that this omission (iron technology and urbanisation in the Ganga valley) is related to the overall brahmanical bias of the framers of the *NCF*, for, the phenomenon of urbanisation and the formation of kingdoms in the mid-first millennium BCE is linked to the rise of new religious ideologies that challenged Vedic thought.

Similarly, cataclysmic social changes, viz. the rise of the numerous *varnasamkaras* (mixed castes) in the five centuries between *circa* 200 BCE and *circa* 300 CE on account of the persistent questioning of the brahmanical fourfold varna order and the arrival and absorption of such forces as those of the Shakas, Kushanas, Parthians, Indo-Greeks, etc. did not find any allusion. The only point of emphasis in this context seemed to be guided by the notion that these post-Mauryan powers were invaders who accepted one or other Indian religions. Indeed, the concerned unit supposed to be dealing with social life as reflected in contemporary literature (*circa* 200 BCE and *circa* 300 CE) went to the extent of dropping all references to caste. Strangely, students were to learn about the four stages of life (*ashramas*) without being told about varna.[7] It is intriguing that this period, which is the one for which there is a large corpus of inscriptional and archaeological evidence, was to be taught only on the basis of the Dharmashastras, Smritis, Sangam texts and what was vaguely referred to as other literature. Also, from the way the literary sources were listed, one got the impression as if the Buddhists and the Jains were illiterate. That this period was perhaps one of the most dynamic periods in terms of art, with major centres in Mathura and Gandhara, as well as an extremely vibrant period of the growth of urban centres is not even hinted.

In the 'Secondary Stage" (classes IX-X) the pre-Modern history of India was reduced to something called the 'Heritage of India' incorporating both 'natural and cultural'. However, while mentioning 'Tradition; Art, Craft and Aesthetics; Architecture; Literature; Science and Technology; Unity in Diversity' under 'cultural heritage', there was absolutely no indicator of the role of the society in creating such a heritage. Whose heritage is sought to be preserved? The question remained unanswered. The focus only on Varanasi, Patna and Allahabad remained unintelligible. There are many other crafts centres with more viable historical continuities, which do not find any mention, e.g. bead making in present-day Cambay, that might have links with some Harappan techniques of bead-making, or, the craft of silk weavers in Kanchipuram, or the construction of catamaran boats – so essential to coastal economies in south India. It is ironical that destroyers of the Babri Masjid were talking about 'preserving heritage'. *Nau sau chuhe khake billi haj ko chali*!

Almost the entire syllabus of the medieval period of Indian history was clothed in the framework of political history. Here too, except for a very stereotypical formulation, viz., 'social and economic conditions' it was more than obvious that social history was considered eminently dispensable. The entire approach is the old colonial approach. Echoing the paradigm of 'dark ages' argued by Vincent Smith and earlier colonial historians, India after Harsha – post 7th century CE – was described as a period of small kingdoms. Again, following the old colonial pattern, the coming of the European Companies is put in a separate unit, instead of being integrated into units dealing with the region or the period, i.e., South India (16th century), Jahangir and Shah Jahan (17th century). To emphasize Hindu resistance, Aurangzeb's conflict with the Afghans was not even mentioned.

'India in the 20th Century' forming part of class IX syllabus sought to enable the learner to understand contemporary India in the light of world developments and to appreciate the fact that people of India, irrespective of religion, caste, gender and region participated in the struggle for freedom. And yet, there was no reference to fascist organisation (the Rashtriya Swayamsewak Sangh) in juxtaposition to 'Fascism and Nazism' as developments preceding the Second World War.[8] The exercise is replicated in the formulation of 'growth of communalism and partition of India' for the syllabus on Modern India for Class XII. It was crystal clear that the motive here is to introduce a communal bias in the teaching of history. The primary effort was directed towards teaching that communalism was born and existed in India only in the form of Muslim communalism. While the Muslim League is mentioned the Hindu Mahasabha and the RSS are not.[9]

The *NCF*[10] almost vowed to take students 'towards an indigenous curriculum'. No wonder, history syllabi makers diligently worked towards what may be called edifying history. Talking about the greatness and glory of a nation is perhaps the easiest way of teaching history. True, there are many worthy things about India, which prompted A.L. Basham to write *The Wonder That Was India*. But there were very ugly things too: casteism, entrenched social inequalities and power hierarchies, oppression of the shudras, *antyajas* (modern day Dalits), religious factionalism, rampant superstition, extreme gender discrimination, and so on. India's interaction with the world was important. For instance, during the Middle Ages, India received a great deal from the Arab world in administrative systems, land and revenue management, music, architecture, chemistry, medicine, even couture. Similarly, it gave a great deal to the rest of Asia and Europe. Understanding all this, and grappling with the reality of *sati*, widespread illiteracy, or tyrannical village life, requires *confronting*, not censoring, the past. We can dispense with such an understanding of the dialectics of history writing only at our peril. The *NCF* and history syllabi based on it suppressed such complexities. It reinforced motivated prejudices of what the renowned E.P. Thompson had once called a 'deformed mind': "Deformed culture was more destructive than atom bombs and a deformed mind was the ultimate doomsday weapon. Culture is deformed when Reason/Rationality wilfully divorces itself from moral sensibility and awful realisation clobbers human imagination to death. Consequently people learn to first kill 'the Other' in abstraction long before the first stone is hurled."

III

CBSE Notification (2001)

An administrative fiat from the Director (Academic) of the Central Board of Secondary Education, Delhi in October 2001 directed "All Heads of Institutions affiliated to CBSE" to immediately comply with the directions notified by the NCERT to the effect that "certain portions and statements from the history books of various classes published by them

(NCERT) have been deleted with immediate effect" and that "these portions and statements are not to be taught in respective classes or discussed in the classroom..."[11] To set the record straight, the aforesaid circular of the CBSE mentioned ten passages from textbooks of classes VI, VII and XI. Of these, eight pertained to the ancient period and one each to the Sikhs and the Jats in the 17th and 18th centuries. Displaying a meek compliance that stands at variance with its statutory power to set and supervise school syllabi, the autonomous Central Board of Secondary Education (CBSE) did not provide any explanation for this extraordinary purge. However, in a written explanation of his decision, Dr. J.S. Rajput, the then Director of the NCERT argued rather speciously that the organisation had "been fighting court cases against certain communities which have felt hurt by some of the contents in history books." This had led him to accede to the demand "by various groups and sections of people to ensure that there are no biased and hurtful statements in NCERT books." It is also well known that the immediate provocation for the NCERT's extraordinary step was a storm that was raised in the Delhi State Assembly by Congress legislator Arvinder Singh Lovely about the supposed denigration of Tegh Bahadur, revered by the Sikhs as a guru of the faith.

Some of these passages dealing specially with important issues of social history may be cited *in extenso*:

(1) "The Varna System: Religion influenced the formation of social classes in India in a peculiar way. In other societies the duties and functions of social classes were fixed by law which was largely enforced by the state. But in India varna laws enjoyed the sanction of both the state and religion. The function of priests, warriors, peasants and labourers were defined in law and supposed to have been laid down by divine agencies. Those who departed from their functions and were found guilty of offences were subjected to secular

punishments. They had also to perform rituals and penances, all differing according to the varna. Each varna was given not only a social but also a ritualistic recognition. In course of time varnas or social classes and *jatis* or castes were made hereditary by law and religion. All this was done to ensure that vaishyas produce and pay taxes and shudras serve as labourers so that brahmanas act as priests and kshatriyas as rulers. Based on division of labour and specialisation of occupations, the peculiar institution of the caste system certainly helped the growth of society and economy at the initial stage. The varna system contributed to the development of the state. The producing and labouring classes were disarmed, and gradually each caste was pitted against the other in such a manner that the oppressed ones could not combine against the privileged classes.

"The need of carrying out their respective functions was so strongly ingrained in the minds of the various classes that ordinarily they would never think of deviating from their dharma. The *Bhagavadgita* taught that people should lay down their lives in defence of their own dharma rather than adopt the dharma of other others, which would prove dangerous. The lower orders worked hard in the firm belief that they would deserve a better life in the next world or birth. This belief lessened the intensity and frequency of tensions and conflicts between those who actually produced and those who lived off these producers as princes, priests, officials, soldiers and big merchants. Hence the necessity for exercising coercion against the lower orders was not so strong in ancient India. What was done by slaves and other producing sections in Greece and Rome under the threat of the whip was done by the vaishyas and shudras out of conviction formed through brahmanical indoctrination and the varna system."[12]

(2) "The people living in the chalcolithic age in south-eastern Rajasthan, western Madhya Pradesh, western Maharashtra and elsewhere domesticated animals and practised agriculture. They kept cows, sheep, goats, pigs and buffaloes, and hunted deer. Remains of the camel have also been found. But generally they were not acquainted with the horse. Some animal remains are identified as belonging either to horses or donkeys or wild asses. People certainly ate beef, but they did not consume pork on any considerable scale."[13]

(3) "The cattle wealth slowly decimated because the cows and bullocks were killed in numerous Vedic sacrifices."[14]

(4) "In fact, for special guests beef was served as a mark of honour (although in later centuries *brahmans* were forbidden to eat beef). A man's life was valued as equal to that of a hundred cows. If a man killed another man, he had to give a hundred cows to the family of the dead man as a punishment."[15]

(5) "The brahmanical reaction began as a result of the policy of Ashoka. There is no doubt that Ashoka adopted a tolerant policy and asked the people to respect even the brahmanas. But he prohibited killing of animals and birds, and derided superfluous rituals performed by women. This naturally affected the income of the brahmanas. The anti-sacrifice attitude of Buddhism and of Ashoka naturally brought loss to the brahmanas, who lived on the gifts made to them in various kinds of sacrifices. Hence in spite of the tolerant policy of Ashoka, the brahmanas developed some kind of antipathy to him... Obviously they were not satisfied with his tolerant policy. They really wanted a policy that would favour them and uphold the existing interests and privileges. Some of the new kingdoms that arose on the ruins of the Maurya empire, were ruled by the brahmanas..."[16]

The excision of these and several other passages clearly reveal that in its concern for religious sensibilities, the NCERT had decreed not only a yawning vacuum in students' understanding of vital phases of early Indian and later medieval Indian history, but had also left no one in doubt that it could not care less about the need to develop scientific temper by encouraging reasoned enquiries into the understanding of historical processes. The 'objectionable' portions were at odds with Hindutva's brahmanical version of history which glorifies India's past and presents it as a series of 'Hindu' achievements, unmatched anywhere else. Crucial here is the tailoring of truth to specific prejudices. The proponents of such a view of history were also miffed with passages which said that there was no archaeological evidence of an ancient settlement around Ayodhya, and that the 'earliest inscriptions' in Mathura did not attest Krishna's presence. This runs counter to the literal, superstitious belief that Rama and Krishna were actual historical figures (rather than mythological ones). A section seeking to place the Jain *tirthankaras*[17] in a historical context was also deleted since it tried, in accordance with accepted historical methodology, to unravel the mystique that surrounds prophets in narratives of the faith. It is almost as if the NCERT had decreed that mythological time cannot be cast in chronological terms, that received religious legends should be impervious to the inquiring mind. It should be a matter of serious concern that a chapter on "modern historians of ancient India", which provided an extended treatment of the various approaches and methodologies in the study of history, also suffered for its suggestion that "rational" analysis that cut through the fog of religious revivalism was a vigorous tradition in India.[18]

The purging also meant that students would not know anything about the material life of the people of the chalcolithic farming cultures in south-eastern Rajasthan, western Madhya Pradesh and western Maharashtra, who had taken giant strides in cultivating extraordinary varieties of crops. Further, in pandering to the sensibilities of the Sikhs, not only the author's criticism of Aurangzeb's action of Guru Tegh Bahadur's execution but also Guru Govind Singh's effort to create a strong regional power in the Punjab have been struck off. This deletion has left a gaping hole in the historical understanding. It is as if the Sikhs had no existence in medieval India from 1658 onwards. The NCERT's move also seems to sanctify a dangerous view of history as a quarry that can be mined to settle contemporary political scores.[19]

The vile prejudices underlying the censorship episode make nonsense of the very idea of education, which has to do with cultivating the mind to think critically, understand complexity, and value truth. The CBSE fiat separated those who see history as a truthful account of reality, which demands continual reinterpretation, from those who yoke history to narrow 'nation-building' agendas inculcating irrational national 'pride'.[20]

IV

NCF-05

The National Curriculum Framework, 2005 (hereafter, *NCF-05)* was adopted by the Central Advisory Board of Education in September, 2005. It is a massive document of 124 pages, which is rather loud on words. It is also a deceptively challenging document in so far as it shirks the responsibility of identifying the source of the accumulated 'critical mass of discomfort' that is supposed to have provided 'a special ignition' for those who got involved in its preparation.[21] It may be recalled that the unconstitutional *NCF*, 2000 trying to bulldoze the skewed notion of fragmented nationalism, was solely and squarely responsible for creating this nation-wide 'discomfort'.

The *NCF* had laid quite some focus on 'The Child as a Constructor of Knowledge'.[22] Reiterating it, the 2005 Document, too, recognises that all children are potential 'knowledge creators'. Further, it also puts considerable emphasis on language education and knowledge creation. We have elsewhere discussed the implications of such formulations.[23] Presently, however, we would like to draw attention to only two major specificities that impact the writing of history. First, absence of any space for reason as the basis of knowledge construction and second, the phenomenal thrust on 'local knowledge' and 'local belief systems'.

Granted that feeling, intuition and experience do provide bases for 'knowledge'. But where is the space for reason, rationality, scientific spirit and 'information' based thereon? Why is 'information' seen as antithetical to 'knowledge'? The document leaves no one in doubt that 'local knowledge' and 'local belief systems', rather than the scientific spirit constitute 'a rich storehouse of information.'[24] As an after thought perhaps the *NCF-05* concedes: 'However, all forms of local knowledge must be mediated through constitutional values and principles' (this proviso was missing in the original draft). If enactment of laws and expressions of pious hopes through such provisions were enough, India would have become a reasonably egalitarian society free of sectarian rivalries rooted in hatred, prejudices and discriminations of varied hues long ago. The Constitution abolished untouchability and forbade 'its practice in any form' through Article 17. The Parliament, too, passed the Untouchability (Offences) Act about half a century ago (1955) [made more stringent and renamed the Protection of Civil Rights Act, 1955] to implement Article 17. And yet, the nation witnessed the celebration of the Golden Jubilee of these enactments through the burning of scores of Dalit houses in Gohana (Haryana) and Akola (Maharashtra) in 2005. Ritualistic invocation of relevant provisions of the Indian Constitution can neither substitute for the paramount need for an adequate space for the voice of reason in the domain of history writing, nor help in bridging several social divides perpetuated by the *NCF*.

The *NCF- 05*'s disdain for a space for reason in school curricula is bound to have a very regressive impact on history writing for children in the impressionable age ranging from 11 to 17. The contours of history writing generated through the *NCF* are already before us. Regretfully, however, textbooks (sorry, we should start calling them reference works, for, the *NCF-05* is determinedly anti-textbook culture) on history are shrouded in mystery, for, the authors of these books are apparently working under an oath of secrecy. Obviously, such a beginning is truly in conformity with the pattern already set in the post-*NCF* mould. Notwithstanding this ominous beginning, the signals available in the history syllabi of the three stages of school curricula under *NCF-05* make us apprehensive that books written under the current NCERT regime might also end up buttressing and/ or avoiding such motivated prejudices as have already been underlined in the post-*NCF* history syllabi.

Coming back to the thrust on 'local knowledge' and 'local belief systems', the question requiring serious consideration would be: where and how does one draw the lines of the 'local', 'supra-local', 'regional' and 'national'?[25] Some of these notions have entered the vocabulary of history writing in recent decades, but with considerable vagueness. Presiding over the tenth session of the Punjab History Conference in 1976, Professor Romila Thapar had raised this problem when she argued: 'One might begin with the historical point at which the awareness of being a region and having a history, is first expressed.... The question of boundaries has its own complexities since man-made boundaries change frequently and rapidly with each political change. The only stable boundaries are geographical and even these are liable to be substantially modified by ecological changes. The definition of a region requires the co-relation of many facets in the study of historical evolution...'[26]

Semantic complexities apart, we are strongly apprehensive that reposing the utmost and an undiluted trust in the 'local' to the level of making it a 'belief system' may cause serious havoc in history writing in general and social history in particular. Here, we would like to remind ourselves of Edward Said's brand of 'indigenism'. Inspired by it, Ronald Inden could only produce *Imagining India* (first published in 1990 at the height of the Ayodhya movement) with an unabashed plea for the 'hegemonic Hindu state' clothed in neo-colonialist, communalist and racist strains, e.g., frequent allusions to 'the Dravidian mind' and such gems of wisdom as 'Hindu kingship was the constitutive institution of Indian civilisation,' 'collapse of Hindu kingship' was brought out by the 'Muslim Turks', which in turn, led to the formation of 'caste', 'Hinduism epitomises the 'Mind of India' and 13th century conquest of north India by 'Muslim Turks' heralded 'the mind that is made to preside over the divisive Middle Ages, which is not the mind of the west – of will governed by reason' and so on.[27]

The concern for the 'local' as a pedagogical strategy, in times when children in the United States are getting their lessons in English from tutors located thousands of kilometres away in Kochi in India, is perhaps far more antithetical to the 'reason-based knowledge' than the assumption that 'information' is antithetical to 'knowledge'. The *NCF-05* formulation is: 'The tendency to confuse knowledge with information must be curbed'.[28]

Take a look at the following classroom situations where the 'local knowledge' and 'local belief systems' would form the bases of the construction of the child's 'knowledge': [a] schools in Tamil Nadu: According to the decree of the four Shankaracharyas, the Adi Shankaracharya was born on April 3, 509 BCE ; [b] children in Rajasthan being told that along the great river Saraswati were Kapalmochan and Ranmochana where 'the Pandavas took their bath'; and that practices such as *jauhar, sati* and *parda* were results of the evil Muslim influences; [c] schools in Godhra teaching through textbooks underlining that the *varna* system was a precious gift of the Aryans to mankind; [d] thousands of Vidyabharatis and Shishu Mandirs all over India telling their young students that the entire pre-Ghorid period of Indian history was the Vedic period, the Kaba in Mecca is in fact a Shivalinga, and all foreigners, including Christians, are anti-national; [e] children in madrasas being told that the sole criterion for considering kings as good or bad is to see if they are/are not 'god fearing', and 'from Harappan seals it appears that people were making different deities as partners of Allah'[29]; [f] children in Gohana (Haryana) sharing their local experience derived from the inscription scrawled on the back of a lorry: *buri nazar wale tere ghar mein ladkiyan paida ho* (you evil-eyed people, may girls be born in your home).

The *NCF-05* would justify the perpetuation of all such myths, prejudices of caste, religion and gender, based as they are, after all, on the 'local knowledge traditions'. One wonders if this enthusiasm for the 'local' is something like the brahmanical tradition of recognising the primacy of the *shruti* (supposedly divine oral tradition) over the *smriti* (written tradition).

Given the post-modernists' view of the 'national', it is only to be expected that growing communalisation of the society, polity, and more significantly of education is a non-issue for its practitioners. The remarkable silence of *NCF-05* on this issue is perhaps not a coincidence. If the *NCF* was a document of fragmented nationalism, that of 2005 can be expected to reduce the 'nation' to a mere metaphor in the glorious style of the Chicago Manual.

V

NCF-05 AND HISTORY SYLLABI

The syllabi of courses released for the teaching of history in the Upper Primary Stage (Classes VI to VIII), Secondary Stage

(Classes IX and X) and the Senior Secondary Stage (Classes XI and XII) have religiously provided the necessary flesh to the structure and philosophy of the *NCF-05*. Many of the concerns and objectives of the history syllabi have been clothed in vocabulary reminding us of the exercise undertaken in the post-*NCF* phase. In the latest formulation, these include:

- Historical sensibility/sensitivity/awareness.
- 'Learn to think historically'.
- Interconnections between processes and events.
- Histories of different groups and societies.
- Interact actively with source material.
- Sensitise students to question of gender.
- Histories of different regions/different communities and different ways of life.
- Histories of displacement/marginalisation as much as processes of development.
- Each theme in the syllabus could draw on examples from a different region for close study.
- It is perhaps not a mere coincidence that the overall conception of and attitude towards history syllabi and history writing in both the *NCF*s share a common concern for reducing the load on children.[30]

The entire conception of history seems to be resting on some kind of romanticisation of the discipline – reducing it to a mere narrative of episodes. *One looks in vain for any thrust on studying elements of change and continuities in historical processes, which are so vital for an analytical understanding of the subject. The need to focus on an explanation of historical phenomena is equally conspicuous by its absence.* If one were to take clues from the semantics of various formulations, the preponderance of the occurrence of 'story' in the various rubrics of the class XII syllabus could not be a mere coincidence. It seems to have almost become an obsession.[31]

The invocation of the notion of multiplicity of 'Pasts' is

understandable. However, giving the nomenclatures of 'Our Pasts-I', 'Our Pasts-II' and 'Our Pasts-III' is clearly an indicator of the hesitation to enter into the debate on tri-fold periodisation of Indian history into 'ancient', 'medieval' and 'modern', which would have involved interventions in the socio-economic processes.

Obsessed with the concern to reduce 'load'/'burden' of students, provisions of themes have been made in such a manner that both students and teachers will have the option of leaving out more than 60 per cent (10 out of 16 themes) of the curricula of the formative Secondary Stage (Classes IX and X). It is proposed to study India in relation to the 'Contemporary World' during the two years of this stage. For each year, three units have been identified in an identical manner as Unit I: Events and Processes; Unit II: Economies and Livelihoods; and Unit III: Culture, Identity and Society. Since three themes each are given under Units I and II and only 'two themes from the first two units' need to be studied in each year, it is more than likely one of these units may not be taught at all. What a way to reduce the students' burden! It needs reminding ourselves that in the syllabi prepared under the *NCF*, too, teaching of medieval Indian history got a short shrift ostensibly to lessen the 'burden' of students!

Class VI–VII syllabi set out their objectives as introducing students to strategies of (a) analysing material culture, (b) textual analysis, (c) political expansion, (d) military control, and so on. One wonders if archaeological fundamentalism resting on the debunking of India's rich literary history is also a strategy.[32] This is typified in the studied silence on 'Vedic literature'. Notwithstanding the growing interests in studies on manifestations of material life, one may still ask if the remains of skeletons are going to tell us if they were those of brahmanas, kshatriyas, vaishyas and shudras!

Apparently, in order to focus on the theme of culture

and identity, an evasive mentality seems to be at work, specially in formulating rubrics on Indian history. Thus, in class X, the student would get his lessons in colonialism and nationalism through 'the story of cricket' rather than through de-industrialisation and Dadabhai Naoroji's 'Drain of Wealth'. Assuming that 'the attempt to make students aware of the fact that everything – clothing or food, sports or leisure, print or books – has a history' is a laudable objective, complete absence of any reference to the process of de-industrialisation (it is not mentioned even once in the entire history curricula for Classes VI-XII) under the British colonial regime is a clear case of underplaying Western imperialism.

Another example of evasiveness may be seen in coping with issues of social tensions and social disparities, class exploitation, peasants' struggles, etc. Amongst several objectives, one reads about concern for 'histories of displacement/marginalisation.' But what does one see in actual implementation? In formulating the syllabus for class VI, where students would receive their first lessons on the ancient period of Indian history (euphemistically called 'Our Pasts-I), the word 'caste' does not figure at all and its first occurrence takes place perhaps in the context of the Mughals. Tribes and nomads are sprinkled here and there but one would look in vain for any reference to the shudras, unless it is assumed that student would be told about them under the rubric 'The Vedas and What They Tell Us' (class VI). What the October 2001 Circular of the CBSE sought to achieve by implementing the NCERT directive to delete passages from history textbooks, is being replicated by such conspicuous absences in defining parameters of social history. No real flesh has been provided for sensitising students about the dynamics of Indian society in general and that of the role of women in particular. In the true 'gender history', as it has come to the fore in the last fifteen years, women are seen not merely as additional players but as primary players. For instance, it is not enough to say that women were respected in a particular period. That Gargi Vachaknavi was perhaps a highly erudite scholar may be conceded. But can we ignore that her rival and contestant sage Yajnavalkya asked her to shut up lest her head was chopped off? Must we not reflect on the stereotypical descriptions, where the supposedly 'exalted', 'honourable' position of women is identified through rubrics such as *ardhangini, grahalakshmi* and the *dharmapatni* – all male-derived categories? Further, a recent study of some Upanishadic narratives highlights that 'stories' of women's quest for 'higher knowledge' (as in the case of Maitreyi) represented 'crises of wives and mothers'.[33]

Further, the hesitation to mention the RSS and the Muslim League is another manifestation of the carefully designed strategy of absences. The word 'communalism' first occurs in the syllabus of class XII ('Themes in Indian History') under the Unit entitled 'Partition through Oral Sources'. It needs to be underlined that notwithstanding the well known links between the RSS and the Nazis, the former are not mentioned even in the class IX curriculum, where the thrust is on studying India in relation to the 'Contemporary World' and a separate theme of the 'Rise of Nazism' has been provided. This silence/absence is characteristically similar to the one already noticed in the *NCF* and its accompanying history syllabi. And this coupled with soft pedalling of Western imperialism is a heady mixture which is also common to both the *NCF*s.[34]

One of the objectives of the syllabi for the 'Upper Primary Stage' is spelt out as: 'Create a sense of historical diversity. Each theme would provide a broad over view, but would also focus on a case study of one region or a particular event. ***In choosing the case studies the focus would shift from one region to another,*** so that the diversity of historical experiences can be studied without over burdening the syllabus.'(***emphases added***). Apart from the vexed problem of defining 'region' mentioned above, at times there is quite some mismatch between the theme and the concerned case study. To illustrate: one fails to understand the link between the case study of Tamil Nadu and the theme of 'second urbanisation' (class VI). Similarly, the concern for displaying interconnections between processes and events remain a mere pious hope – its best example is the avoidance of debating the role of iron technology in the emergence of 'second urbanisation', which reminds us of the similar positioning in the syllabus of 2000. Arbitrary inclusion of various regions can hardly be regarded as giving attention to regional history. In terms of social processes, one would like to think that a proper regional history would be concerned with the interface of the regional and the mainstream and with a study of how the region contributes to the mainstream.

Absence of sensitivity towards non-Sanskritic and anti-brahmanical cultural strains was indeed conspicuously displayed in the *NCF*, in its accompanying history syllabi, in the CBSE Order and subsequent textbooks produced by the NCERT.[35] Regretfully, the 2005 history syllabi also does not inspire much confidence on this score as well. Let us illustrate this.

In the Punjab, the social stratification based on the brahmanical four varna order presents its own problems. brahmanas rarely play a dominant role in the society of this region (notwithstanding Kosambi's theory of origin of brahmanas going back to the pre-Vedic times, i.e., the Harappan civilisation during which modern day Punjab was part of that phase). The kshatriyas fade out after a while and the khatris, who often claim to be kshatriyas, are invariably associated with professions more akin to those of the vaishyas. The intermediary orders of kshatriyas and vaishyas are absent in Bengal, too.

Several Tamil inscriptions of the medieval era have revealed the existence of a social formation, which had emerged as a challenge to the hierarchical caste system based on brahmanical ideology. The social formation called *valangai* (meaning Right Hand) and *idangai* (Left Hand) was made up of lower classes, consisting mostly of artisans, merchants and hill-tribe soldiers. The groups were of horizontal nature and they had existed for nearly five centuries (10th to the 14th, specially under the Cholas). Though the two groups were against the hierarchical system, there was caste hierarchy within each group. Evidently, the anti-brahmanical movement of the E.V. Ramaswamy Naicker in the early 20th century had a much deep rooted ancestry.

In several textbooks the life sketch of B.R. Ambedkar is confined to his role as an "architect" of India's Constitution. The serious challenge that he posed to the brahmanical order or his radical conversion to Buddhism as a method of social and political emancipation (10 lakh Dalits were converted to Buddhism on October 14, 1948; on December 25, 1925 Ambedkar burnt copies of *Manusmriti* at Mahad village in Maharashtra – all these are political statements) find scant or no mention at all. Textbooks, through allusion and exclusions strengthen the false claim that in a vast majority of cases these conversions happened under force.

Many conversions to Islam/Christianity in the modern period coincided with the passage of emancipatory laws liberating bonded labour. This allowed oppressed sections the freedom to exercise choice in the matter of faith. Rightly or wrongly, they perceived Islam/Christianity to be more egalitarian than the caste system of the Hindus. For example, the first "low" caste person to walk the public road near the temple in Tiruvalla (Travancore) in 1851 was a Christian. Around the mid-19th century, the struggle of Nadars on the right of their women to cover the upper part of their bodies was opposed by the upper castes. Large scale conversions to Islam on the Malabar coast took place not during the invasions of Tipu but during 1843-90. These were linked to abolition of slavery by the British in 1843 in the region.

It is pity that children are still going to be taught within the parameters of the colonialist paradigm of a static Indian society. Often, the so-called truth is multi-layered. Innumerable examples of dichotomy between the theory of the brahmanical social order and the actual practice varying social relations can only be explained by investigating the actual caste stratification at various historical times and in varied historical regions. Such nuanced social history is missing in the recent attempts to define contours of history writing for school children, including the syllabi released after the *NCF-05*.

There are several questions that make the study of social history meaningful. To illustrate a few: Why did tensions take dimensions of conflict ? What was the nature of conflict between the 'Aryans' on the one hand and *dasas, dasyus, panis*? Was it racial or a case of cultural maladjustment? What was the process by which the Greeks and Scythians came to be called *vratyakshatriyas* and how were they assimilated into Indian society? How did the people of the 13th century view the Arabs and Turks? Were they just 'Muslims' for them?

The contribution of forest dwellers, tribes, peasants, pastorals and other groups to the formation of Indian culture are generally ignored in existing textbooks. The definition of Indian cultures cannot be restricted to upper social strata, its 'Hindu' articulations, and has to consider the contributions of other castes, communities and religions. The emergence of new religions and the role of established religions can be better understood if their historical and social contexts are kept in view. Religions have to be taught not merely in terms of scriptures and doctrines and that too with the avowed objective of pronouncing superiority of one over the other.[36] Rather, they should be looked at more in terms of what led to their emergence and who were their followers. Imperatives of social history demand that there is greater probing of the levels and intensity of the success of religious teachers/orders professing to change the face of societies. Why did the Buddha, for example, fail to eradicate social divisions notwithstanding his questioning of its fundamental premises? Did brahmanical temples and *mathas* and non-brahmanical monastic institutions perform only the so-called 'religious' functions or had vested landed interests as well? How did religious sects contribute to proliferation of sectarian caste identities? If we are to appreciate and understand the complexity of Indian society, we must be aware of and reflect on, the range of cultures that make up Indian civilisation. We cannot choose some and denigrate others in an arbitrary fashion. The post-*NCF-05* syllabi have lost an important opportunity to make the study of social history challenging.

VI

Extracts

Here, in this section, we have chosen a few extracts or summaries thereof from textbooks of different hues and from different regions, which were produced in the last two decades. The Bipan Chandra Committee (1986-92) had surveyed history books used in schools of Uttar Pradesh, West Bengal, Madhya Pradesh, Andhra Pradesh, Assam, Kerala and Tamil Nadu. Its Report was submitted in 1992. It clearly underlined the direct link between the level of communalism and how history was taught in these seven states.

Some Examples from the Bipan Chandra Committee Report

Andhra Pradesh: "Alauddin Khilji suppressed the Hindus. He wanted to make them as poor as possible. So he collected many taxes from them. He did not allow them to wear good clothes, ride on the horses or chew betel leaves."

Assam: The absence of unity in the "Sepoy Mutiny of 1857" is seen only in terms of Hindus and Muslims not acting concertedly. "While the Muslims were trying to restore power for the Mughals, the Hindus were bent upon giving power to the Peshwas."

West Bengal: "The ninth Guru Tegh Bahadur had established a reign of murder and destruction in Punjab. When he was arrested and brought before Aurangzeb, he claimed that no sword could harm him. At this, Alamgir ordered the executioner to strike him and the result was as was to be expected. His head was severed from his body."

From some textbooks published by the NCERT after 2000

"Vedas prescribe punishment for injury or killing of cow by expulsion from kingdom or by death penalty as the case may be" [recall Jhajjhar (village Dulina) killings of five Dalits skinning dead cows for their living. They were killed by upper caste Jats on Dussehra day in 2000]

A chapter on 'The Vedic Civilisation' in the class VI textbook tells us about the Vedas, Brahmanas and Upanishads without any reference to rivers of the Saptasindhu (Afghanistan) and with a focus only on the Ganga, Yamuna, Saraswati, Indus and Sutlej, and does not make any distinction between "early" and "later" Vedic in describing "political conditions" and "economic life". Further, we are told that "Kings were democratically elected by people" and their duty was "promotion of the people's well-being and progress"; "there were rules which governed the debate and behaviour of members in the Sabha and Samiti like our parliament" (sic). "Father's property was inherited by all children."

An extract from the rape report of the National Commission for Women

"In India, in ancient times, women had enjoyed an able position in the household and in society. As the "queen" of the household, her position was envied by her counterparts elsewhere. Unfortunately, constant invasions by foreign elements from about the 8th century changed the scenario to the detriment of women. Her vulnerability to abuse by the invading hordes bestowed upon man a responsibility to protect her and from thence developed the inherent dominant role of the male within the family fold and her inevitable dependence on the male."[37]

Extracts from textbooks used in Gujarat[38]

'The varna system was a precious gift of the Aryans to the mankind... the responsibility for the miserable plight of untouchables lay with their illiteracy and not in their exploitation and oppression by the higher varnas.

Demonising non-Hindu religions a textbook says: "Apart from the Muslims, even the Christians and Parsees are foreigners. In most states the Hindus are in minority and Muslims, Christians and Sikhs are in majority." In several books the Christian priests of Middle Ages are deliberately denigrated with descriptions of Christian churches, calling them part and parcel of the feudal system of exploitation with their own impositions of taxes, fees, selling miracles, etc. While such descriptions are historically true, the blatant bias does get reflected in complete silence about equally exploitative brahmana priests in India during the early medieval centuries known for their feudal tendencies. Don't they hold Dalits to ransom even today?

Amongst 'Customs of the Rajputs' we get to read that 'The Rajputs occupy a special place in Indian history – they were the last Hindu kings in Indian history; Rajput women enjoyed freedom in society ... the birth of a female was considered bad omen in the family...It was considered a virtue to perform *sati.*'

The *Sanskriti Gyaan* and *Gaurav Gaathaa* series used in the chain of Vidya Bharti Schools and Saraswati Shishu Mandirs run by the RSS are designed to promote bigotry and religious fanaticism in the name of inculcating knowledge of culture in the young generation. Some specimens betraying utter lack of historical sense and known for carrying a highly motivated socially divisive agenda are:

(a) India was the "Original Home of World Civilisations" – the first people to inhabit China and Iran were Indian Aryans.
(b) The languages of the indigenous people (Red Indians) of the northern part of America were derived from ancient Indian languages.
(c) The conspiratorial policies of Christians were responsible for the 1947 Partition. Even today, Christians in Nagaland, Meghalaya, Arunachal Pradesh and Kerala are anti-nationals.
(e) Jesus Christ roamed in the Himalayas and drew his ideas from Hinduism.
(f) Mahapadma Nanda had so much wealth that if divided among the population, every person would get Rs. 50 lakhs.
(h) Child marriage, *jauhar, sati, purdah, jadu-tona* and superstition were all due to the fear of the Muslims.
(j) In the Vedic period "there existed no state, no king, no penalty and no criminal, all protected one another by virtue of dharma." [never mind the *Rigveda* mentioning gamblers and a father selling his son for 100 cows, etc.] "The best description of dharma is to be found in Manu.
(k) "Some divine power, whether it was Bhagavan Rama or Krishna, has always emerged for preservation of greatness of Indian culture. The Hindu organisation RSS has arisen to end the present miserable condition and for the defence of the greatness of Indian culture — Bharatiya sanskriti."

The task of writing social history is being made increasingly difficult because the bogeys of parochial, sectarian and hurt religious feelings are being invoked too frequently. In the process, several Holy Cows have been created in different parts of India. Some years ago, a move was afoot in Rajasthan to ban G.N. Sharma's *Mewar and the Mughal Emperors*, which had been a well known and very popular textbook for undergraduate courses since the 1950s. The reason — suddenly, some organisation decided that its discussion of Maharana Pratap hurt the religious sentiments of the 'Hindu Rajputs'. Similar pleas have often been invoked in case of Chatrapati Shivaji — it is becoming impossible to write anything critical about him in Maharashtra.[39] It sounds funny, but it is disturbing to learn that in some colleges in Maharashtra, Shivaji is being taught without reference to Aurangzeb. An analytical article on the cult of Swami Narayan by Ghanshyam Shah invited considerable wrath against him in Gujarat in the early 1990s. A CD ROM on Mahatma Gandhi issued under the auspices of the Information & Broadcasting Ministry of the Government of India (of the NDA Government) did not even mention Nathu Ram Godse as the killer of Gandhi.

Lucien, the Greek satirist and a Sophist, while lampooning the historians of his times (2nd century CE) said: "Objective history has no favourites and manipulating history appears to be, now, the official pastime". How prophetic he was. I can't help recalling in this context Sir Shafaat Ahmad Khan, the First President of the Indian History Congress (the Congress was then known as All-India Congress of Modern History), who addressed the historians in 1935 thus: "I dread the prospect of long lines of histories of India written by Muslims, Marathas, Sikhs, Bengalis and Pathans, each from their own point of view. Should history be tied to the chariot wheels of perverted sectionalism which is now acting as a most serious obstacle to the growing nationalism of India as a whole?" Don't these words uttered more than seventy years ago sound too contemporary?

Historians cannot allow the historical discipline to degenerate to the extent that the distinction between myth and history is lost and false history becomes instrumental in promotion of political mythology. The *raison d'etat* of history teaching and writing is reason and not faith. If historians are forced to tailor history writing to suit narrow sectarian, political and ethnic interests, we would soon have only histories of/by and for the Hindus, Jains, Sikhs, Muslims, Parsis, Marathas, Dravidians, but no history of India — India as known for thousands of years — multi-religious, multi-ethnic, multi-linguistic, multi-cultural, a pluralistic India.

NOTES

(**) This is a slightly revised version of 'Whither Social History?' It was delivered as the General President's Address at the Thirty-eighth Session (March 18-20, 2006) of the Punjab History Conference held at the Punjabi University, Patiala. See *Proceedings* of the Conference (2007), pp. 6-35. A complementary presentation on the theme and its wider ramifications is our contribution 'Scientific Communication and History Writing' — Paper presented at the First Peoples Education Congress held at Allahabad in September 2005 and published in N.P.Chaubey and Sushma, eds. *Science Communication*, Peoples Council of Education, Allahabad, 2009, pp. 142-85.

1. *NCF*, p. 32.
2. Ibid., p. 9.
3. Ibid., Section 3.8.1, pp. 89-90. The Vocational Education and Training (VET) Programme envisaged in *NCF-05* (pp. 110-12), too, has many parallels with the aforesaid understanding. Its vision of honing 'skills in crafts' through ITIs, polytechnics, Krishi Vigyan Kendras, rural development agencies, etc. also imply that these would largely be catering to the dire needs of the socially disadvantaged groups in a somewhat caste-oriented manner. A carpenter's child can only hope to be a better skilled carpenter. An upward mobility would perhaps remain a vain hope for such children. This is hardly a recipe for obliterating caste divides. Nor does this help in bridging the rural-urban divide as is also noticeable in the following.
4. *NCF* - section 5.1.2, pp. 108-9.
5. Ibid., Section 1.4.7, pp. 18-20.

6. Ibid., Section 2.8.3, pp. 53-4. Speaking about language education, *NCF-05* (p.35) says: 'In the non-Hindi states, children learn Hindi. In the case of Hindi states, children learn a language not spoken in their area. Sanskrit may also be studied as a Modern Indian Language in addition to these languages'. Why this special accent on Sanskrit? How and when does Sanskrit graduate from being a classical to 'Modern Indian' language (notwithstanding its listing in the Eighth Schedule of the Indian Constitution)? One wonders if the present formulation is inspired by the aforesaid formulation of *NCF*.
7. No wonder, in some textbooks we do indeed read blanket statements that *ashramas* were meant for all without any distinction of caste and creed.
8. The class X book on World History in Gujarat has a section called 'Ideology of Fascism/Nazism' where the strong national pride that both these generated, the efficiency in bureaucracy and administration and other "achievements" are detailed but the violent, uncivilized politics of exclusion – of the Jews, trade unions, migrant labourers that did not fit into Mussolini or Hitler's definition of rightful citizen – just do not find any mention. Nor does the extermination of six million Jews in the Concentration Camps, the Holocaust, figure in these texts. Early in March 2001, a Workshop was organized on 'Image of India in Germany and Image of Germany in India in High School Education'. Shri Atul Rawat, who was then a consultant to the NCERT, attended it as the Indian "expert" and trying to ingratiate himself to German experts, said that Hitler and Nazism were still popular in Germany – obviously much to the embarrassment of the visiting scholars. Rawat rubbished the NCERT textbook *The Story of Civilisation,* which was in circulation then and was indeed praised by the Germans for being positive towards their country, for its leftist 'bias' in parts that dealt with Germany. Rawat also said that such textbooks would soon be replaced by "correct" ones. One was left under no illusion that he had plans to "correct" the books along the lines of Gujarat textbook on World History. Would such forces, as have been represented by Rawat, and those behind drafting post-*NCF-05* syllabi, learn some lesson from the recent episode

of David Irving, the Nazi apologist and revisionist British historian, who has been sentenced to jail in Austria for rubbishing the Holocaust as "a gas chamber fairy tale"? See also note 34 below.

9. Jawaharlal Nehru, the first Prime Minister of independent India, had in his several writings between the 1930s and the early 1950s, constantly warned about destructive potentialities of communal forces of both Hindu and Muslim hues and their close affinities with Fascism of the Nazis. He wrote in 1936: "It should never be forgotten that communalism is the development of recent days and it has grown before our eyes." Nehru considered communalism a petty bourgeois incident and continuously underlined that it only fulfilled vested interest of landlords, zamindars, businessmen and moneylenders. On December 7, 1947 he wrote: "We have a lot of evidence to show that Rashtriya Swayamsewak Sangh (RSS) is an organisation, which is like a private army and definitely marching on the path of staunch Nazis, it is even employing their techniques." And in August 1948 he wrote: "The method employed by the RSS is to speak in a sweet tongue but their ideology and activities are quite different and just contrary to the ideology which has guided us for centuries." Again writing in December 1948 he said: "To compromise with something, which is undoubtedly an evil, is always dangerous. Everything that the nationalists stand for is a direct target of the RSS movement." His statement of October 1951 has been extremely incisive and enables us to reflect on developments since the early1980s. He had then written: "All sorts of social reactionary forces are behind these communal organisation. Some of the old rulers who are out of power but are very rich, jagirdars, big zamindars and some big capitalists support these communal organisations and they vehemently talk of Hindu rule, Sikh state and ancient Hindu culture. They conceal their secular intolerance and reaction under the cover of ancient culture. These communal organisations are essentially fascist in terms of ideology and technique." Its pity that both the *NCF*s have shown remarkable apathy towards such a disastrous force – almost making it a non-issue. For a handy access to some of the writings of Nehru cited here, see 'Nehru's Struggle against

Communalism' in *Nehru Yuva Sandesh,* Monthly News Magazine of the Nehru Yuva Kendra Sangathan, Ministry of Youth Affairs and Sports, Government of India, November 2005, pp. 10-12.

10. *NCF*, Section 2.3, p. 37.
11. Circular No. 24 No. DIR(A)/HIST/2001/12932-19431 dated October 23, 2001.
12. Ram Sharan Sharma, *Ancient India* (textbook for class XI) chapter on "Legacy in Science and Civilisation" pp. 240-1.
13. Ibid., p. 45.
14. Ibid., p. 90.
15. Romila Thapar, *Ancient India* (textbook for Class VI), pp. 40-1.
16. Ram Sharan Sharma, op.cit., pp. 137-8.
17. Ibid., chapter on "Jainism and Buddhism", pp. 91-2.
18. Ibid., On "Types of Sources and Historical Construction", pp. 7, 20-1.
19. This has reference to the deletion of passage on Jats conducting "plundering raids" in Arjun Dev and Indira Arjun Dev, *Modern India*, chapter on "India in the Eighteenth Century", p. 21. See also note 37 below.
20. It is remarkable that the forces behind the CBSE directive are active in carrying on similar campaigns beyond the frontiers of India. The Rashtriya Swayamsewak Sangh (RSS)-linked organisations put their stamp on school textbooks in California in the United States. The State Board of Education, California, has been engaged in approving the history/social science textbooks for grades six to eight in schools, an exercise undertaken periodically. The Hindu Education Foundation and the Vedic Foundation (based in the US) have used the occasion to push through "corrections" in the textbooks approved. The "corrections" demanded by the Hindutva organisations are integral to the Sangh Parivar's political agenda in India, and similar to what the NCERT did during 1999-2002 in respect of the *NCF* and textbooks in social sciences, particularly history. For example, among the "corrections" suggested, there is a clear attempt to deny the integrality of the caste system in ancient India. "The Vedas came to form the major beliefs of the religion called Brahmanism" is replaced with: "The Vedas constitute the source of Hinduism". Early Aryan religion is to be replaced

with references to early Hindu religion. On women, it was suggested that the references to gender bias in ancient India were incorrect and insulting to Hindu society. Therefore, the line, "Men had many more rights than women" was to be replaced by, "Men had different duties (*dharma*) and rights than women. Many women were among the sages to whom the Vedas were revealed." The current Hindutva preoccupations such as asserting the sacredness of cows, vegetarianism and the Saraswati civilisation myth have also found their way into the textbooks. The references to technology, science and mathematics in ancient India have been modified to enable suitable glorification; and negative aspects of society are either deleted or presented as cultural specificities rather than as oppressive ones.

The concerted campaign of Hindutva forces against textbooks in California schools also raises a very fundamental question, viz., are histories of a community or religious groups to be written only by members of such groups? The Hindutva organisations have taken the position that non-Hindus cannot write the 'correct' history of Hindus. There was a campaign on the Internet to stop Jesuit Fr. Francis X. Clooney from visiting India in 2005 – his tenth trip to India since the early 1970s. The world-renowned expert of Purva Mimamsa, Vedanta, Sri Vaishnavism and comparative theology had just been appointed Parkam Professor of Divinity and Professor of Comparative Theology at Harvard University. The attack on Clooney was only one of the many attacks directed at Western scholars studying Indian religions. Broadly coinciding with the rise of the Hindu Right in Indian politics, the majority of these attacks have their provenance on the Internet and have emanated from bodies associated with the VHP. Since the late 1990s, the targets have included some of the most respected names in religious studies in the US Academy–Wendy Doniger, who holds multiple appointments in the University of Chicago; Paul B. Courtright, Professor, Department of Religion, Emory University; Jeffrey J. Kirpal, J. Newton Rayzor Chair in Religious Studies, Rice University; Sarah Caldwell, formerly Assistant Professor of Religious Studies, California State University, Chico, and Visiting Professor at Harvard Divinity School; and David Gordon

White, who teaches at the Religious Studies Department of the University of California, Santa Barbara. For a detailed exposition of this tirade against non-Indian scholars writing on India and Hinduism, see Krishnan Ramaswamy, Antonio de Nicolas and Aditi Banerjee, eds., *Invading the Sacred: An Analysis of Hinduism Studies in America*, Rupa & Co., New Delhi 2007.

21. *NCF-05*, p. iv.
22. *NCF*, Section 1.4.13, p. 26.
23. Cf. 'Another Retreat of Reason', *Frontline*, October 7, 2005, pp. 47-9.
24. *NCF-05*, p. 29.
25. In one of the strongest endorsements of the document, Professor Shahid Amin ['Ride the Learning Curve', *The Hindustan Times*, September 1, 2005] had made a strong plea for studying the 'local'. More than that, he has pitted it against the 'national', as if the two are mutually exclusive.
26. Romila Thapar, 'The Scope and Significance of Regional History', *Proceedings of Punjab History Conference*, 10th Session, Patiala, 1976 (1977), p. 14.
27. For a critique of Edward Said's brand of 'indigenism' and its construction by Ronald Inden see Krishna Mohan Shrimali, 'Reflections on Recent Perceptions of Early Medieval India', *Social Scientist*, Vol. 21, Number 12, December 1993, pp. 25-39.
28. *NCF-05*, p. 96.
29. Communalisms of different hues feed one another. Books being used in *madrasas* in north India are no less incisive as far as the fate of teaching and writing of history is concerned. The National Steering Committee on Textbooks Evaluation undertook a review of books of several states for the NCERT. In its Report of 1993, it brings out several stereotypes in the reconstructions of Islam in books in use in West Bengal. A Report (*India Today* : June 25, 2001) on the drive to "purify" education spearheaded by the Barua Rahamani Education Society (an organisation of Islamic leaders with Saudi Arabian ties and operating since the early 1990s) describes 109 *madrasas* being run by the Society in West Bengal. The President of the Society is quite candid in saying : "The Islamic consciousness of our children is stifled in the state-controlled *madrasas*".

Aurangzeb and Mahmud Ghazni are portrayed as heroes and all their actions are justified. While the network of 109 schools being run by the Society is no match to more than 20,000 schools of the Sarasvati Shishu Mandir and Vidya Bharati; the objective and methodology are easily comparable. Hatred runs through the common agenda.

30. *NCF*, p. 62: "In order to make the social sciences education meaningful, relevant and effective, the concerns and issues of the contemporary world need to be kept in the forefront. To this end, the quantum of history may have to be substantially reduced." Elsewhere the *NCF* talks about careful deletions of "redundant portions of information in the existing curriculum ...so that the exercise may not result in any additional load for the learners." [p. 32. See also the Section 1.4.12 'Reducing the Curriculum Load', *NCF*, pp. 25-6]. Compare this with the introduction to 'Social Science Syllabus' under the *NCF-05*: 'Textbook writers will be concerned to ensure that understanding does not suffer through suffocation of details'. Amongst objectives of history teaching and writing for the 'Upper Primary Stage' (classes VI-VIII, where all students shall be reading the entire Indian history) we read about focusing on creating 'a sense of history' and studying 'diversity of historical experiences' 'without over burdening the syllabus'. This concern for reduction of load is somewhat baffling. Both the *NCF*s are marked by contradictory signals. While the *NCF-05* is clearly allergic to the 'textbook culture' and yet argues for 'plurality of textbooks'. One fails to understand the logic of the argument that children should be encouraged to use multiple textbooks in a subject along with dictionaries and reference works, particularly when the guiding principle of *NCF* is '*Learning Without Burden.*' The earlier *NCF*, too laid down that the teaching / learning should not be confined to the textbooks alone and the pupil should have access to reference materials on the subject in the library...'[Rationale of history teaching at senior secondary stage].
31. Obsession with 'story' may be seen in the following formulations in class XII syllabus:

    Story of the First Cities: Story of Discovery: Harappan Civilisation.

Political and Economic History: How Inscriptions tell a story: Story of discovery.

Social Histories: Story of Discovery: Transmission and publication of the *Mahabharata*.

A History of Buddhism: Sanchi Stupa: Story of Discovery of Sanchi Stupa (Incidentally, History of Buddhism is to be taught only through Sanchi stupa! Why not Amaravati, Nagarjunakonda and several others in Andhra Pradesh?)

Story of Discovery of *Ain-i Akbari*.

Story of Discovery: Account of the production of court chronicles, and their subsequent translation and transmission.

Story of Discovery: Account of how Hampi was found (for the entire medieval period including the Sultanate and the Mughals, architecture is to be understood only through Hampi.

Story of Transmission: How Bhakti-Sufi compositions have been preserved.

32. We do not share the scepticism displayed by scholars *vis-à-vis* literary and archaeological sources. Some Indian archaeologists (for example, Dilip K. Chakrabarti, *Colonial Indology: Socio-politics of the Ancient Indian Past*, Munshiram Manoharlal Publishers Pvt. Ltd., New Delhi, 1997), in their zeal for pretentious iconoclasm, have been debunking India's rich literary heritage (Vedic literature in particular). Similarly, Bruce Lincoln in an appendix 'On the use of archaeology in the reconstruction of Indo-Iranian religion' (*Priests, Warriors and Cattle*, pp. 179-84) has been quite dismissive of archaeological evidence and maintains that the study of proto-Indo-Iranian religion rests mainly on 'linguistics, mythic reconstruction and so on'. Such compartmentalised reconstructions are often too blinkered. Castigating 'archaeological purists', Raymond Allchin and Bridget Allchin (*The Rise of Civilization in India and Pakistan*, Cambridge University Press, Cambridge, 1982, p. 354) emphatically asserted: 'To admit such a restriction would, in our view, make a nonsense of our aim of reconstructing the rise of Indian civilization, since it would rule out a large and most interesting part of the evidence.' Historical processes need to be studied through multifarious angles and with data from diversified sources. The relevance of Kosambi's 'Combined

Methods in Indology' (reproduced in D.D.Kosambi, *Combined Methods in Indology and Other Writings*, compiled, edited and introduced by Brajadulal Chattopadhyaya, Oxford University Press, New Delhi, 2002. This anthology has been reviewed by us; cf. 'The Making of an Indologist', *Frontline,* September 13, 2002, pp. 72-4), in this context, is too obvious to be stressed. See also Romila Thapar, *Cultural Pasts: Essays in Early Indian History*, Oxford University Press, New Delhi, 2000, Section III: Archaeology and History. In a devastating critique of Chakrabarti's notion of history and methods of history writing reflected in his *Colonial Indology*, B.D. Chattopadhyaya ('Confronting Fundamentalisms: The Possibilities of Early Indian History', *Studies in History*, Vol. XVIII, No. 1, January-June 2002, pp. 106-12) identifies them as 'archaeological fundamentalism' which suggests 'a dangerous, uni-dimensional nationalist agenda of writing about the past.'

33. Yohanan Grinshpon, *Crisis and Knowledge: The Upanishadic Experience and Storytelling*, Oxford University Press, New Delhi, 2003, *passim*. See also Krishna Mohan Shrimali, *Knowledge Transmission: Processes, Contents and Apparatus in Early India,* presented at the Symposium on 'Education and Transmission of Knowledge in Indian History' held at the 71st session of the Indian History Congress on February 12, 2011 and published as Symposia Paper No. 26 by the Congress. Brian Black's *The Character of the Self in Ancient India: Priests, Kings, and Women in the Early Upanishads*, State University of New York Press, Albany, 2007 is also an enlightening work insofar as it underlines the potentials of Upanishadic 'stories' as historical evidence.

34. In January 2006, the Parliamentary Assembly of the Council of Europe voted to condemn the "crimes of totalitarian communist regimes", linking them with Nazism and complaining that communist parties are still "legal and active in some countries." It would be easier to take the Council of Europe's condemnation of communist state crimes seriously if it had also seen fit to denounce the far bloodier record of European colonialism – which only finally came to an end in the 1970s. While there is precious little connection between the ideas of fascism and communism, there is an intimate link between colonialism and Nazism. The terms *lebensraum*

and *konzentrationslager* were both first used by the German colonial regime in south-west Africa (now Namibia), which committed genocide against the Herero and Nama peoples and bequeathed its ideas and personnel directly to the Nazi party. Up to a million Algerians died in their war for independence, while controversy now rages in France about a new law requiring teachers to put a positive spin on colonial history. Comparable atrocities were carried out by all European colonialists, but not a word of condemnation from the Council of Europe. Presumably, European lives count for more. Whose interests are being served by underplaying Western imperialism and colonialism and maintaining studied silence on Indian fascism by the makers of the two *NCF*s and subsequent history syllabi?

35. Max Mueller was known for his the antipathy towards non-Sanskritic components of Indian culture. In his *India What Can it Teach Us?* he categorically stated: "Language of the sacred writings of the Buddhists and Jains was borrowed from the vulgar dialects." Such colonialist perceptions have not been questioned by the modern day 'cultural nationalists'. In the chapter on the Gupta empire in a textbook produced by the NCERT in 2002, the thrust is clearly on popularity of Vaishnavism, Shaivism and development of Sanskrit literature. There is no reference to Buddhism and Buddhist art—not even to the Sarnath Buddha—a 'classic'/ 'masterpiece' of Indian art. Reference to the feudal growth, urban decline and decline of money during the so-called 'golden age' of Indian history are also conspicuous by their absence.
36. A typical example of such a construction is Chapter 17 entitled 'Major Religions' in the textbook (*India and the World*) on Social Science for class VI release in 2002 (after *NCF*), where the history component has most probably been authored by Dr. Makkhan Lal. We had extensively reviewed this chapter in 'Faith Accompli' published in *The Hindustan Times* dated November 16, 2002. It has been reprinted in *Saffronised and Substandard : A Critique of the New NCERT Textbooks* published by SAHMAT, New Delhi, 2002, pp. 61-4.
37. This extract is almost a mirror reflection of the description of women in a textbook of Pakistan: 'Islam gives respect to all

women ... They are considered mothers, wives, daughters and sisters. Prior to the advent of Islam, a woman's status was that of a slave or servant. Islam gave women human rights and the right to inheritance. ... Islam has determined woman's status. A Pakistani woman...is not suffocated like women in traditional Hindu society. She is looked upon as the Queen of the Home. Heaven lies about her feet and this is an important concept.'

38. Analysed and reported in *Communalism Combat* (October, 1999). The trend we have been witnessing in other states of the communalisation of the government school system in the last decade is much older in Gujarat.
39. James W. Laine's *The Epic of Shivaji* was banned by the Maharashtra government in January 2006 as it is said to have contained "insulting, tasteless, objectionable writing with a *mala fide* intent about Shivaji and his parents". Laine's book *Shivaji: Hindu King in Islamic India* was banned in January 2004 raising similar reasons. Ironically, Laine did not write *The Epic of Shivaji.* It is a direct translation of *Shivabharat*, a Sanskrit text written by Kavindra Paramananda. The reasons for the ban, however, are less to do with Shivaji's history and more to do with political manoeuvres. For a detailed report on this issue, see Anupama Katakam and Nandagopal R. Menon, 'Politics of a Ban', *Frontline,* February 24, 2006, pp. 93-7.

About the Authors

VIKAS GUPTA has been an Assistant Professor in the Department of History, University of Delhi since 2007. Prior to that, he worked for four years as a Social Science teacher in government schools in Delhi. His area of research includes themes in the history of colonial education; social aspects of knowledge 'production' and 'reproduction'; and neoliberalism and its impact on the creation of inequalities in contemporary education. He has published numerous articles in leading journals such as *Economic & Political Weekly, Seminar, Mainstream, Proceedings of the Indian History Congress*, etc. He has also delivered lectures at various nationally and internationally renowned academic centers. He is the Associate Editor of *Reconstructing Education* — quarterly publication of the All-India Forum for Right to Education (AIFRTE). Presently, he is working on a monograph on school education, where he is exploring the transition from colonialism to neoliberalism and how the mainstream education system could be reconstructed to nurture and promote pluralism and equality. He is actively associated with AIFRTE, Dilli Shiksha Adhikar Manch (DSAM) and Sambhavana Organization which are striving for the universalisation of education of an equitable quality.

Email: vikasedu@gmail.com

MAHIMA SINGH has been an *alumnus* of two renowned institutions of the University of Delhi. Having obtained her Bachelor's Degree in History Honours with a First Class from the Lady Shri Ram College (popularly known as LSR), she went on to do her postgraduation in History from St. Stephen's College. She has worked as a Faculty Assistant with the Vidya Bhawan Education Resource Centre, Udaipur (Rajasthan), a non-profit resource organization that works towards reforming public education. She has collaborated with educationists and resource personnel from several state education boards to help develop curricula and material for history teaching-learning (Grades VI-X). She utilized her training in the 'Early Indian Art and Architecture' to pursue an Elite Programme in Cognitive Semiotics and earned a postgraduate certification in Cognitive Semiotics of Visual Art from the University of Aarhus (Denmark). She is currently doing an internship with the Bellevue Arts Museum, Seattle (USA), acquiring experience with museum education for school children and adults.

Email: mahimasingh87@gmail.com

SMITA SAHGAL is an Associate Professor of History, Lady Shri Ram College (University of Delhi). An *alumnus* of St. Stephen's College — she completed both graduation and postgraduation in History from this renowned institute of the University of Delhi. After her doctoral thesis on *Bull Cults in North India: A Socio-Religious Study* up to *c*.500 CE (University of Delhi), she has just completed a post-doctoral research project (sponsored by Indian Council of Historical Research) on *Niyoga: Commissioned Procreation and Sexual Regulation in Early India – A Socio-Historical Study in North India between 1500 BCE and 700 CE*. Author of more than a dozen research papers published in prestigious journals (*The Indian Historical Review, Social Science Probings, Proceedings of the Indian History Congress, Women's Watch*, etc.), her interests range from gender studies to religious explorations within Jain religion and Brahmanism. In 2006, her research paper on Polyandry was awarded the Indian History Congress Prize (Ancient India).

Email: smitasahgal16@yahoo.com

PRADEEP KANT CHOUDHARY is an Associate Professor of History, Deshbandhu College (University of Delhi). He has a first class Master's Degree in History from the University of Delhi. With a teaching experience of more than 22 years at the undergraduate and postgraduate levels in the University of Delhi, he is known for his monograph *The Cult of Parashuram: Study in the Making of an Avatara* (2010) and translations of half a dozen seminal works of History into Hindi. Currently, he is engaged in a project related to the study of *Village Shrines and Deities of North Bihar.* He is keenly interested in various aspects of the rural life and challenges of its development. He works with an organization called ANADI (Act Now for Alternative Development Initiative) which provides consultancy to the common people in rural Bihar to enhance agricultural productivity. He is also involved in the field of rural primary education to improve its quality and supports low cost school initiatives in Bihar.

Email: pkcdu@yahoo.com

SHALINI SHAH is an Associate Professor in the Department of History, University of Delhi. An *alumnus* of St. Stephen's College — she completed both graduation and postgraduation in History from this renowned institute of the University of Delhi, securing a first class in the Master's degree. She has worked for nearly 25 years on issues of gender relations in early India and female sexuality, and has published many research papers in prestigious journals such as *Studies in History, The Indian Historical Review, Indian Journal of Gender Studies, Social Science Probings, Women's*

Watch, Wellcome History, etc. She has worked on texts of different genres, viz., Dharmashastriya, Kamashastriya and even medical treatises from a gendered perspective. She is the author of such pioneering monographs as *The Making of Womanhood: Gender Relations in the Mahabharata* (Second Revised Edition, 2012) and *Love, Eroticism and Female Sexuality in Classical Sanskrit Literature: Seventh-Thirteenth Centuries* (2009).

Email: shalini64_shah@rediffmail.com

K.M. SHRIMALI retired as Professor of History, University of Delhi in September, 2012 after serving the University for over 44 years, of which 13 years were spent at St Stephen's College, his *alma mater*. Some of his important publications include: *History of Panchal* (in two volumes); *The Agrarian Structure in Central India and the Northern Deccan: A Study in Vakataka Inscriptions; Constructing an Identity : Forging Hinduism into Harappan Religions; Dharma, Samaj aur Sanskriti; The Iron Age and the Religious Revolution.* Amongst several monographs edited by him are: *Essays on Indian Art, Religion and Society* (1987); *Archaeology Since Independence* (1996); *A Comprehensive History of India,* Vol. IV (jointly with Professor R.S. Sharma, in two parts). Currently, he is working on a multi-volume *Dictionary of Social, Economic and Administrative Terms in Indian Inscriptions* (a project of the Indian Council of Historical Research) and 'Geography of Early Indian Religions: An Exercise Towards Atlas of Early Indian Religions' (under Senior Academic Fellowship of the Indian Council of Historical Research). He has been associated with the activities of several leading organisations and academic bodies of professional historians and archaeologists and is committed to the dissemination of scientific and secular history through the teaching and writing of history – both at the academic level as well for common people.

Email: kmshrimali@yahoo.com